T0275116

Praise for Sara Sherbill's
There Was Night and There Was Morning

"Sherbill masterfully explores the fragile bonds of family and faith with courage and clarity. . . . She illuminates how darkness can coexist with compassion, how a father's shadow cannot extinguish a daughter's light."

—Alyson Richman, international bestselling author
of *The Thread Collectors* (with Shaunna J. Edwards)
and *The Lost Wife*

"Fiercely brave, eloquent, and brilliant in its evocation of a family teetering on the brink of catastrophe shrouded beneath religious devotion and the myth of perfection, *There Was Night and There Was Morning* is nothing short of a tour de force. Sara Sherbill has expertly crafted a harrowing story of truth and transcendence that will stay with me forever."

—Elissa Altman, author of *Motherland*

"A haunting account of family, abuse, faith, and survival. In her poignant debut memoir, Sherbill examines her childhood as the daughter of a rabbi who led his congregants with grace but terrorized his family with his temper. . . . Sherbill's lyrical style gives just enough detail to keep readers grounded without overwhelming the narrative's broad scope. . . . A poetic story about one woman's search for redemption of faith and family after abuse."

—*Kirkus*, starred review

"Can prayers, if not well-kept, grow holes and spoil? What happens when rituals that keep us safe also betray us? After all our prayers have forgotten us, how can we learn to pray again? Sara Sherbill's *There Was Night and There Was Morning* is a spellbinding memoir that lays what is holy bare."

—Sabrina Orah Mark, author of *Happily*

"Searing and vulnerable, this heartbreaking story reads like a pre-war memoir of Jewish life, its seasons and rituals and sensations. But at its center lies a dark and timely undercurrent, which coincides with our post–#MeToo moment. As the history of a father and rabbi's hidden life of addiction and abuse emerges, Sara's courage, honesty, and refusal to compromise her integrity as a daughter, mother, and writer, will leave you awestruck."

—Ariel Burger, author of *Witness: Lessons from Elie Wiesel's Classroom*

An unflinching, deeply affecting account of family, faith, and abuse. This book brings us close to the devastating ways in which a family can come apart and, at the same time, is a testament to the redemptive power of telling your own story."

—Tova Mirvis, author of *The Book of Separation*

There Was Night
and There Was Morning

There Was Night and There Was Morning

A MEMOIR OF
TRAUMA AND REDEMPTION

Sara Sherbill

**UNION
SQUARE
& CO.**

NEW YORK

UNION SQUARE & CO.

NEW YORK

For Nicky

"God saw all that he had made, and it was very good.
And there was evening, and there was morning—the sixth day."

—Genesis 1:31

CONTENTS

PART I

Honor Your Father and Your Mother

1 The Sabbath Queen.. 3

2 The Still and Quiet Afternoon.................................... 12

3 My Eyes Are Closed, But I'm Still Listening 23

4 The Letter 37

5 Girls Who Aren't Praying 49

6 You Could Learn a Thing or Two from Your Daughter 65

7 A Woman of Valor, Who Can Find?........................... 75

PART II

You Shall Have No Other Gods Before Me

8 All the Glory of the King's Daughter Is Within.......... 95

9 The Dead Sea 115

10 Sounds of Joy and Gladness.................................... 131

11 You Are My Angel... 153

12 Welcome to Miami.. 167

13 That's Your Story, Not Mine.................................... 189

14 One Little Goat.. 209

15 The Beginning of Compassion.................................. 229

16 The Unbinding of Isaac... 239

17 Apocrypha.. 251

Acknowledgments... 259

PART I

Honor Your Father and Your Mother

1

THE SABBATH QUEEN

WHEN I WAS YOUNG, I loved being a rabbi's daughter. I loved the prayer books' silken pages, the slightly raised ink of the letters. I loved baking challah with my mother on Friday mornings, leaving enough time for the dough to rise and the bread to bake before sundown. I loved my book of Bible stories with the pictures and the pictures in my head, which were more vivid and majestic than anything in a book could ever be: the Red Sea splitting, Moses descending the mountain with two stone tablets, God in his throne, listening to our prayers.

I loved the synagogue's red velvet seats, the men's cream-colored wool prayer shawls, the cantor's voice of supplication. I loved my mother's Shabbat candlesticks with their melted, dried wax stuck in the silver handiwork, the weekly rush and quiet, the dishes and silverware, the guests and the chocolates they brought, which we ate after the prayer over the wine, after the prayer over the bread, after the meal, after the singing, after dessert, but before the Grace After Meals.

I loved the silver goblets filled with wine that everyone must sip from, the apples dipped in honey at the beginning of the new year, the fried potato pancakes during Hanukkah when it was cold outside and night came early, the Passover Seder, when I got to stay up until midnight, my eyes closing as I sat on my father's lap, exhausted from the hour and from the sweet, dark wine my father permitted me to drink.

When I was young, my teacher at Sunday school told us that God is everywhere, and I believed that was true, but that was before I discovered that God can disappear, that God can turn His face, go into quiet hiding, and that even though He is everywhere, you may have to work the rest of your life to find a trace.

On Friday mornings, I helped my mother bake challah for Shabbat, the Jewish Sabbath, which began Friday night at sundown and continued until Saturday after dark. I stood next to her on a stool, wearing my red-flowered apron, and watched her knuckles sink laboriously into the elastic dough, its fleshiness turned over and over beneath her delicate fingers, yielding a smell that was alive with yeast and comforting with home.

I knew that challah dough could become sticky with kneading and that it required frequent dustings of flour to keep it supple. My mother would say, "Sara, I need more flour now," and she would lift up the doughy sphere so that I could sprinkle the flour, which seemed to me like a special kind of angel's dust, onto the counter space beneath. I smoothed it delicately over the Formica surface, the yellow moon suspended in my mother's hands.

When Friday night arrived, my father went to synagogue, which we called, in Yiddish, *shul*, though nobody in my family spoke Yiddish—not even my mother's father or my father's mother, both of whom seemed more American to me than my parents.

"Give Abba a kiss goodbye," my mother said, using the Hebrew word for father, one of only a handful of Hebrew words in her vocabulary outside of the prayer service, which, though she knew it well, she didn't understand. "When Abba comes back, it will already be Shabbat."

My father left for shul before the Sabbath began so that he could drive there. Once Shabbat started, no use of electricity was permitted, according to Jewish law. No turning on and off lights, no cooking, no driving, no television, no radio, no telephone. Other Shabbat laws meant no writing, no use of money, no baths, no bicycles, no drawing, no carrying anything outside.

By the time my father left, I had already had my Shabbat bath, which meant I got to use my mother's special green soap that came in a tall green plastic bottle and that had to be held upside down and squeezed in order to release its dark liquid, so green it seemed black. The soap smelled like pine, which in turn smelled like my mother. Because I was almost six, she sometimes let me squeeze the bottle myself, but I usually squeezed out too much, and it was from Jerusalem, which I knew to be the holiest place in the world, and very far away. It was also the place where my parents had met and where I had been born, though we had left when I was a baby, and I knew it only from stories. My mother squeezed out the soap for me onto a rough brown tool she called a loofah, which I thought was the Hebrew word for sponge.

Then she'd say, "Stand up, Sara, honey," and as I stood knee-deep in the bathwater, she would scrub my legs and arms, especially my knees and elbows, my shoulders and my back until my whole body was slick with a thin green gloss. She told me this was very good for my skin, even if it stung a little.

"Now you'll glow like the Shabbat Queen," she said.

I slinked back into the water to rinse off and also to swim like a dolphin, which I sometimes thought I was. It would have been easier to imagine if our bathtub was white, like at my cousins' house, which lent the water a blue cast, as though it were an inlet in an ocean.

Instead, our tub, along with all the bathroom tiles, was avocado green, making the bathwater a murky and forbidding hue. Still, I would have stayed in the bath forever, if not for my mother telling me that if I didn't get out in time, I wouldn't be able to kiss Abba goodbye before he left.

Sometimes I'd say to my mother, "Ima, wrap my hair up like you do after your bath," but she would tell me my hair was too short and didn't need to get wrapped up. So sometimes, secretly, when she thought I was getting dressed in my room I would stand in front of the mirror and try to wrap my hair up, but I could never get the towel to stay, and then my mother would be calling me, telling me to hurry, that Abba would soon be leaving.

I had special dresses only for Shabbat. In the winter, I usually wore the one with small, dark-colored roses and a big lace collar. I had another with black, dark green, and burgundy stripes and a matching sash, which was my favorite word. I also had a white satin blouse with pearl buttons and a high-neck collar that went underneath a navy wool jumper with big silver buttons and a knife-pleated skirt, sent to me by my grandmother from New York in a big Bloomingdale's box. In the summer, if we weren't having guests, I was allowed to wear my white camisole, which was my second-favorite word, with pajama bottoms.

I put on a Shabbat dress, and I brushed back all my hair, which made me feel very clean, and I felt so proud to be clean for Shabbat and to smell like my mother, who, in turn, smelled like Jerusalem, I was sure. I ran to the door, and my father picked me up and gave me a kiss and said, "I'll be back soon."

∾

While my father was gone, my mother and I set the table, with many extra places for the guests and even extra for the people my father might invite that night. We did not use the everyday dishes; we used the once-a-week Shabbat dishes with their heavy cream centers and golden vine edges. The silverware for Shabbat was also heavy, and I would have liked to set the table slowly, stopping just to feel the weight of it in my hands. But the sun was setting, and the chicken soup was simmering on the stove, and the challah was warming in the oven, and my mother was putting the lights on timers and asking me to put away my markers on the floor as my baby sister played with a rattle on the rug. Everything was speeding forward but poised to stop suddenly at the set time. Every piece of furniture, every bowl and plate, every lamp and pillow, was racing toward the same goal, which kept coming closer and closer, until we lit the candles and everything came to a halt.

My mother had two candles in her tall silver candlesticks. In front of hers were my two candles, set in my small candlesticks. My mother wrapped her hair in a blue silk scarf, differently from the way she wrapped her hair after a bath, and this time, I got to wrap my hair in a scarf too, which my mother tied at the back of my neck. My mother lit her candles, then she lit mine. She used one match for all four candles and never seemed to get scared when the flame ate up the match and crept close to her fingers. We held our hands up in front of our faces and then moved them from the candles to our eyes in three flowing motions. My mother explained to me that this was how we welcomed the Sabbath Queen.

We said the blessing over the candles; then my mother put her hands very tightly over her eyes and swayed back and forth, and her lips moved, but no sound came out. I tried to imagine what she might be saying, but I understood it was not something I could ask about. My mother was very serious then, and if I had tugged on her sleeve, or even if my baby sister had started crying from her crib, where she was sleeping, she would have ignored us. I guessed she was talking to God, and I swayed back and forth and made my lips move with no sound coming out, so I could talk to God too. Sometimes my mother would cry, and to be like her, I cried too. Then she would hold my face in her hands and kiss both my cheeks and say, "Good Shabbos." She would take the scarf off my head, and if she had been crying, she used the ends of her scarf to dry her eyes, the blue silk darkening in spots like deep water.

While we waited, we read books, or I told her about what I was learning at school. When my father came home with the guests, we all sat down at the table, and Shabbat really began. My parents never made a separate kids' table, like they did at my cousins' house, because they knew I liked to sit with the adults and help my mother and answer my father's questions and listen to everyone talk after the other kids had gone downstairs to play.

My mother brought the two challahs out from the oven, gleaming with heat and egg-yolk glaze. She placed them at the center of the table, beneath the white challah cover embroidered with Hebrew words I couldn't read. I had learned in Sunday school that the two challahs symbolize God and the Jewish people, and that we keep them covered so that they don't feel embarrassed that the wine is blessed first.

As my father held the wine goblet in his hand, my mother gleamed like the warm, shiny face of her challah, except even more beautiful. The wine overflowed, dripping down my father's fingers and onto the saucer beneath, a symbol, I knew, of God's kindness. My father began to recite the blessing over the wine:

There was night and there was morning, the sixth day . . . His voice grew louder as he reached the part that thanked God for giving us the Sabbath as a remembrance of Creation.

My father had explained to me the creation of the universe. That God created the sun and moon and stars and all the planets and every living thing. If God created us, I wanted to know, then who created God? My father explained that God had no creator. He was the Ein Sof, the source with no beginning and no end, a power so big we could barely find words to describe it. My father put his hands on my head and blessed me. He asked God to make me like Sarah, Rebecca, Rachel, and Leah, to watch over and protect me, to shine His face upon me. As I stood beneath his hands, I imagined the guests were looking at me, thinking I was the luckiest person in the world.

At first, I was excited we were moving. Since I could remember, we'd been living in a series of small towns near the Iowa border, where all the kids were Catholic. Now we were going to live near my cousins in one of the fancy suburbs on Chicago's North Shore, where there were more Jewish kids my age and where I would go to Jewish school every day of the week, not just on Sundays. We were moving because my father got a job as the rabbi of a new synagogue, but also because my mother wanted to be near her family. We'd be living twenty minutes away from where she grew up, where her brother and extended relatives still lived.

At my new school, my mother told me, I would go to prayer services every morning. There was a little chapel, my mother explained, where all the children prayed together and read Torah on Monday and Thursday mornings from a miniature Torah scroll that had been saved from the Holocaust. I had only the dimmest sense of what she meant by that word, but I knew it had something to do with suffering beyond my comprehension and the "Never Again" sticker on the leather-bound notebook in which my father took notes for his sermons.

I would have two teachers at this school, my mother explained, instead of just one. Mrs. Paley would be my teacher for math and reading, and in the afternoon, Gaveret Ashkenazi would teach us Hebrew and Torah. I marveled at a name as foreign-sounding as Gaveret Ashkenazi.

Stepping into her classroom, I imagined myself entering an alternate reality, a reality I knew about from the picture books my mother read to me before I went to sleep, books where women walked around in kerchiefs carrying eggs in baskets and men wore caps and beards as they pushed wheelbarrows down a dusty road or scurried off to the afternoon prayers.

But, most of all, I was relieved that I would no longer have to explain to the other kids why I couldn't go to their birthday parties on Saturday afternoons, why I couldn't eat the pepperoni pizza, even if the party was on Sunday, and what my father did for a living. It seemed all the kids at school had fathers who were firemen or policemen or something else that was easy to explain. When people asked me what my father was, I'd say, "A rabbi," having learned to add, "It means he's like a priest, but Jewish." Most kids seemed satisfied with this answer, but one day John-Mark Hanson, who was always trying to chase me during recess, said: "If your dad's a priest, how come he has a family? Don't you know priests aren't supposed to have kids?"

I wanted to explain to him that the rules weren't the same for rabbis; that without a family, my father's public role would be empty. Without my mother, I wanted to tell John-Mark, who would light the candles? Who would braid the challah? Who would tell me stories from the Torah? And I knew, without ever having been told, that without me—or my baby sister, or the baby that was just now growing in my mother's belly—my father's life would be lonely and monotonous, his devotion without purpose. But I didn't know how to put into words any of what I wanted to say to John-Mark, so I told him I would have to ask my father, who I was sure would know the answer.

I would be starting second grade in the fall, and my mother told me that, in preparation, I should sit down with a piece of paper and practice writing the alphabet. But I already knew I could do that, so instead I decided to make a list of every word I knew. As I wrote, I began to realize that so many words had variations. Did *tree* count as a separate word from *trees*? Was *walking* worthy of its own entry, distinct from *walk*? I decided the answer to these questions was yes, and the list kept growing until my pink marker ran out and I had to proceed in blue. Even as I wrote, I kept getting distracted, remembering forgotten words. I realized then that there weren't enough hours in the day to record every single word I knew, and that even if there were, by then I would have learned so many new words that I'd have to start from scratch. I realized then that if you tried to record everything you know, everything you think about, and everything that happens to you, and you try to use words to hold it all, you will fail, because the task will become bigger than you, the recording itself will eclipse that which was meant to be recorded and you will ultimately vanish inside it.

It will take years to convince myself that words are not the enemy. That telling this story will not eclipse me. It will take a lifetime to understand that I can record everything I know, everything I think about, and everything that happened to me, and I will not vanish.

2

THE STILL AND
QUIET AFTERNOON

WE ARE EATING LUNCH TOGETHER on a Saturday afternoon. It is almost summer. My dad is at one end of the table, my mom at the other, the rest of us—including my best friend, Eden, who slept over the night before—packed into folding chairs on either side. My father has returned from synagogue, which means he's taken off his jacket and tie, combed his hair back, and changed into a T-shirt bearing the emblem of the youth-group chapter he used to lead. My mother has laid out a feast, each dish glimmering against the dark blue tablecloth like a star in the night sky.

It is, of course, the Sabbath.

We have already blessed the wine, washed our hands twice on each side, and remained silent until we ate the bread; we've already recounted how God created the world in six days and rested on the seventh, already proclaimed the Sabbath a sign forever between the Jewish people and God, when my parents begin to tell the story of how they met. I have heard this story before, but I never tire of hearing it again. The first time my mother met my father, he offered her almonds. She was coming out from between the barracks, nestled among the pine trees, and he was coming at her with his blue eyes and big smile and well-fitted khakis.

"Your mother thought I looked like Paul McCartney," my father says.

"You wish!" she says and starts laughing.

This was in the winter of 1970, on a kibbutz near the Syrian border, where they were both working as volunteers. My mother had been raised in great suburban comfort, with the understanding that one day she would marry a young lawyer or doctor or an heir to a furniture chain. There were any number of eligible young men at the country club she could have chosen from and made her father happy. Instead, she'd gone traveling around the world and found my father, a college dropout from Miami in search of God. At the kibbutz, my mother was assigned to pick grapefruits, my father to run the guesthouse. They were both on their way to somewhere else, in between being the people they had been and the people they thought they could become.

"The thing about him," my mother says, and here she directs her attention to Eden and me, "is that he was a great dancer. And he had tons of tapes. Neil Young, Pink Floyd, the Band."

They would go to work early in the mornings before the sun came up and it became too hot. After work, they'd go hiking in the mountains. "Your father could go down a mountain like a goat," she says.

"I had to teach your mother a lot," he says, and she starts laughing again.

She liked that he was sure-footed, that he could drive a tractor, that he had already mastered Hebrew, having previously taught himself Spanish when he was living in Mexico. At night, they hung out with the other volunteers, from England and Australia and Denmark; everyone had guitars, and they'd play Woodstock albums. Other nights, they'd watch the Katyusha rockets from

Lebanon rain down like fireworks. One time, a rocket hit the chicken coop, and the next morning all the chickens were dead.

My mother wanted to go to India. Some of the volunteers had plans to go soon; others had already been. She wanted to go, and she wanted my father to come too. My father did not want to go to India; he wanted to go to Jerusalem. He wanted to study Torah. He wanted, he told my mother, to become a rabbi someday, but first he would have to study. Like my mother, he came from an assimilated Jewish family. If he wanted to inspire people, he told my mother, to bring them back to God, he needed knowledge. He told my mother she didn't have to look for spirituality in some faraway place. She could look for it in Jerusalem—with him.

One Friday afternoon, they took the bus to Jerusalem, arriving before sundown. At night, they walked to the Old City, to a candlelit apartment where a smiling rabbi was leading people in song. He was talking about joy. The joy of serving the Creator, the joy of knowing where you come from. Men and women, separated by a makeshift curtain, closed their eyes and sang along. If they didn't know the words, they hummed or clapped. Some held babies on their hips or in their laps. My mother had never seen fathers so at ease caring for their children. There was a feeling of contentment in the room, or maybe it was something else—something my mother could not put into words.

I want to hear more of the story—especially the part where my mom leaves for India, then sends my dad a telegram from Istanbul telling him she's made a mistake, that she's making the return trip by boat, that he should meet her at the Haifa port—but I can't because the story's interrupted by my little brothers fighting.

"Joseph's punching me," Ephraim says.

"No, I'm not!" Joseph says.

"You are too!"

"No, I'm not!"

"Boys, stop it," my father says.

"Mom, he's still punching me!" Ephraim says.

I look over at Joseph, who is doing his guilty half-grin.

"Why don't we play a game?" I say.

Eden rolls her eyes. "Oh, Lord, you guys with your games."

It was true. With the exception of my mother, we all loved games. Monopoly, chess, cards, Chinese checkers—it didn't matter. The games were a necessity: the Sabbath constituted twenty-five hours in which we couldn't watch TV or get in the car or talk on the phone. We had always lived apart from the religious community; we did not know anyone else who lived like us. My parents had chosen to live among the assimilated because we were there to set an example.

I suggested we play the category game, which involved picking a category—state capitals, American presidents, tropical fruits, anything really—and going around the table, each person offering an entry, until only one winner remained. It probably wouldn't surprise anyone that the winner was always my father, since he knew everything.

"I don't want to play a game!" my sister says.

"That's only because you always lose," I say.

"We're playing," my father declares. "The category is Beatles songs."

Everyone, except my little brothers, takes a turn, getting the easy ones out of the way first—"Help!" "I Want to Hold Your Hand," "Can't Buy Me Love." Even my sister and Eden know those. We cover the basics—"Lucy in the Sky with Diamonds,"

"Yellow Submarine," "Taxman," "Eleanor Rigby." My brothers have now left the table to play with their action figures.

"'Back in the U.S.S.R.,'" my mother says.

"'While My Guitar Gently Weeps,'" my father says.

"'Dear Prudence,'" I say.

"We've just about covered the *White Album*," my father says.

"What's the *White Album*?" my sister asks.

"What's the *White Album*?" my father says. "What's the *White Album*?" and for a moment I wonder if he really is mad. He turns to my mother and asks, "How can a child of mine ask such a question?"

My mother shrugs.

"It's only the best album the Beatles ever made. Some people think it's *Revolver*, but those people don't know anything about music."

Years later, my mother would tell me there had been a dog on the kibbutz, a little puppy that belonged to one of the volunteers that hung around the volunteer barracks. One day, my mother saw my father kick the dog. Did she see it with her own eyes, or did she only hear about it? Maybe it was a story someone told her. Either way, she knew something wasn't right. But it didn't match up with the man she knew—the man who offered her almonds, the man who wrote her poetry quoting the Song of Songs.

Soon it's only me and my parents left in the game. Then it's just the two of them.

"'I'm Only Sleeping,'" my father says.

"'She's Leaving Home,'" my mother says.

They go back and forth like this, speaking in a language that takes them elsewhere, to a time when she was working in the grapefruit orchards and he was discovering God. It is easy to see how they could love each other, how two people who loved music so much, who *needed* it so much, would recognize that in each other, would know they had found something rare.

Eventually, my mother's knowledge reaches its limit, and my father looks around, shakes his head, and delivers his winning entry: "'And Your Bird Can Sing,'" which he begins to recite in his loud, off-key falsetto.

We are eating lunch together on a Saturday afternoon. It is summertime, and I am ten years old. Eden's not here, and neither is anyone else. Today, there are no guests. It is hot, and my father's come home with his jaw clenched and perspiration on his forehead and under his arms. You know he's in a bad mood because he throws his suit jacket on the couch and yanks his tie off like a snake, and while he does this, he is muttering—you might say he's talking to himself, but it's loud enough so you can hear, loud enough so that you cannot not hear, so maybe he is talking to you too.

Lately, he'd been coming home in a bad mood more and more often. For one thing, the president of the synagogue, Mitch Michaelman, was always trying to undermine him—that was the word my father used, *undermine*. Either Michaelman was bad-mouthing him to the board or else he was thwarting my father's attempts at the latest membership drive. "What does he know about anything?" my father would say. "He's a mid-level accountant. What does he know about reaching people?"

We are at the table, and my mother has just finished bringing out a plate of cold chicken schnitzel, a big bowl of salad, and corn on the cob from the fridge, when my father starts to yell at her—"Is it too much to ask for a warm meal when I get home? You can't do that for me? You won't do that much?"

When it happens, there is no way to go back, you just have to keep moving forward.

"Danny, stop it," my mother says quietly, and he throws a piece of bread at her—bread she baked with her own hands.

It is, after all, the Sabbath.

When he throws the piece of bread at her, my mother says nothing. That is because she believes in defusing the situation. She uses this word with me repeatedly when we discuss my father—*defuse, defuse, defuse.* I don't really know what it means, but I pretend that I do. I cannot keep myself from speaking for her. If she doesn't want me to, who is it that I'm speaking for? If it's me, I am selfish.

Here is where I start screaming. No one makes me scream except me, at least to begin with.

I scream at my father, scream that he cannot yell at her. "Do not yell at her, do not yell at her. Stop being mean," I scream. This is where "Mind your own business" comes in. And I say, "No! I will not mind my own business!" Now chairs are being thrown back, and people are standing up and yelling, and now my mother is yelling too, and my father hits her, and I run. I run to them, not away from them.

I run in between them, jump up and down. I am a monkey on their back, a nuisance not only to my father, as you might expect, but to my mother as well. Underneath whatever it is I am screaming at my father, what I am really screaming is, *Don't hurt her, hurt me, don't hurt her, hurt me don't hurt her, hurt me instead hurt me hurt me hurt me hurt me hurt me instead.*

Now I have made a choice, and now I am being chased around the house. There is plenty of room to run now. I am running to reach my room before my father does, so I can lock the door. It's important to say here that I am afraid. It may sound like a game, but it is not a game. It is nothing like a game.

I get to my room, the room I share with my little sister. She is gone. My two little brothers are gone. My mother is gone. Our house is not big, but on this afternoon, it grows wings and corridors, places to run, to disappear to.

I get to my room before my father and slam the door. I try to lock it, but I am not quick enough. I lean against the door with all the weight of my body. I hope my weight will keep the door closed while I fumble with the lock, but it doesn't. My father pushes the door open, pushes it against me, slaps me down. I get up, run to my sister's bed, because it is as far away as I can get. I stand on the bed, my body pressed into a corner. I have screamed my way into this corner; I scream without words.

My father's blows rain down on me. Now there is less fear, which is mostly about anticipation of what is unknown, and there is pain instead, but I notice that less. Primarily, I feel I am losing my mind, which is what I scream now. I believe in God, and I believe I'm going crazy—I believe this with all of my mind and all of my body, which can still feel the blows.

My father asks nothing of me, except to be quiet. That is all he wants of me, and if you think about it, it is a simple and reasonable request. All he desires is my silence.

Soon my father will go to his room, the room across from mine, the room he shares with my mother, who has quietly vanished. Vanished like a silent piece of glass, a still, quiet light, a gorgeous blankness. Her face turns into a mirror in my head, and I look into it, and I see her as a painting—the painting hanging in her room, the room she shares with my father, the painting above the bed of her mother, a portrait commissioned one year before her death, her face glowing like a bride's face, as though it had retained the beauty she had by that time lost, surrounded by blue gentle light. When I look for my mother's face, this is what I see.

Soon my father will return from his room. He will return with a belt, to finish the job.

My father will hit the bed with the belt. Once, twice, as a warning, so I will not be surprised. It is easy to surprise me, since I am lost in my own terror. By this point, I am no longer afraid of my dad, I am afraid of myself—afraid of my own capacity for noise, afraid of the things I am doing and can't stop doing, like ripping my sister's 1984 World Series poster off the wall and clawing out the thumbtacks with my nails.

My sister was the sporty one, taking after my mother's side of the family. She didn't only like to play sports; she liked to watch them, which is what we did every Sunday at Uncle Peter and Aunt Lily's house—the Bears, the Bulls, the Blackhawks. In most ways, my sister was tougher than me, but when my dad got like this, she knew how to make herself invisible.

I am turned to the wall, and I pray to it with the screams coming out of my mouth, and the sound of them scares me. The wall is white; it will be another two years until my mother and I wipe down these walls with damp cloths, fill the holes in with plaster, and paint them a pale candy pink. But now I am being pulled from the wall like the thumbtacks, and there is a belt coming down on me, and my father's plan has not worked, because somehow I am surprised. I actually am surprised this is happening, even if it has happened before.

Soon the day passes, even if it is summer and a day is a long time. Soon the day will almost be over, and I will go downstairs, maybe after falling asleep, and my mother will be in the kitchen, asking the kids if they are hungry for dinner, nothing fancy, just a small, very late afternoon meal—cut-up peaches and cantaloupe with cottage cheese or even just cut-up avocadoes and tomatoes.

One year, maybe it is this year, our family gets an ice-cream maker as a gift. In the summer, we pour in cream from small cartons, and we put in cut-up strawberries, and there is a handle that needs to be turned for a long time, and there is a very cold metal container you have to hold with a towel because it is too cold to hold with your hand. Sometimes the ice cream comes out good and sometimes it doesn't, but making homemade ice cream is a good thing to do on a hot Midwestern summer day, so maybe that's what my family is doing right now, in this afternoon now being described, when I come out of my room.

My father will be reading the newspaper on the couch in the living room, and there will be only one small lamp on, even though it is almost dark outside. He will be biting his nails, and he will look nervous and afraid. I will also feel nervous and afraid. I will feel whatever he feels.

I will walk past my father—not on purpose, but just because I need to get from the kitchen, where my mom is handing out paper plates to my brothers and sister, to the stairs, so that I can go back up to my room, where I will wait for the dark, whatever it will bring. But as I walk past my father, he will call out to me. Maybe he will use my name and say quietly, "Look at this article in the paper I'm reading—you would be interested in this."

So I will have to go over to where he's sitting. There's no issue of danger or fear or anything like that because this is a different man here. The only thing to fear now is my own sadness and how much of it I can bear until my heart cracks open and all my blood spills out, or else I just die from the weight of the pain I feel for my father.

In the days that come after, there will be words about what has happened. If the bruises are visible, there will be the matter of an apology—something quiet in my room without anyone else there, something under the breath, something I will acknowledge in turn—"Oh, it's okay."

There will be the matter of him closing the door gently behind him, the metal handiwork clicking into place.

My mother will speak to me in the car, on the way to some place. "It's not your fault," she will say; she will say this many times, and it is not until many more years have passed that I will begin to ask questions—questions about geography and location. In years to come, I will say to her, "Our house is not big. How did you get lost?"

For the first days that come after, I wear pants and not shorts, long sleeves instead of T-shirts. For the days after that, there are all kinds of scratches and bruises that come with the summer. Kids falling off bikes, scraping their knees, slipping on diving boards. I'm a girl lost in my own thoughts, I don't watch where I am going, I have never learned to look in front of me, I have never learned to pay attention.

3

MY EYES ARE CLOSED,
BUT I'M STILL LISTENING

I AM IN THE CAR WITH MY MOTHER, driving from one place to another, when she tells me she's pregnant. Right away, I start to cry. What does she expect? Don't I always tell her no more kids?

"I understand that you're upset," she says. "But I hope you'll come to see that this is a good thing for our family. Every child is a gift from God. Every baby brings its own blessing."

But I am not interested in blessings. I am almost eleven, and I am trying to figure out how she could do the things you have to do to make a baby with my father. When we get home, I run upstairs to the room I share with my sister and slam the door and take out my diary and write: "I don't understand how she could have sex with that shithead." I had known about swear words for a while, but had only recently begun using them. I liked the way they made me feel—like I was older than I was, like I had some kind of power I did not have.

I already had two little brothers, Joseph and Ephraim, not to mention my little sister, Rachel. Why did I need more? Did it matter that the house was always messy, that my mom was always yelling, that the caning in the kitchen chairs had collapsed and would never be repaired? That you could open the chest of drawers in the dining room only by pressing your fingertips into the gap where the handle used to be and pulling hard, while balancing yourself at the right angle for leverage?

Ever since we'd moved to Chicago, my dad had gotten worse. So many things at the synagogue made him angry, and that made him angry at us. Now it was not uncommon for terrible words to be thrown everywhere, along with dishes and chairs and a door off its hinge. Every time, I hoped it would be different, but it never was. And yet, the conclusion my mother reached was that what was needed was another child. Another child was the blessing we were missing. Another child would solve everything.

I go into the living room and pick up the phone to call Eden.

"My mom's P.G.," I say.

"Shut up," she says.

"I'm serious," I say.

"This is bullshit," she says.

"No kidding," I say.

Eden knows what I am talking about, of course she knows what I am talking about. Eden has an awareness of just about everything no one else our age has, except for me, which is why we are best friends. It was only last year that Eden's mom had a baby with her third husband, Don, a pockmarked man in beige slacks and a pinkie ring whom Eden and I called crater face. Before that, Eden and her mom had lived at her grandparents' house in her mother's childhood room, where they slept in a pair of twin beds like sisters. Now there was a sprawling ranch house with a pool and a big-screen TV.

"You should sleep over tomorrow night," Eden tells me.

"I don't know if my mom will let me," I say. "It's a school night."

At school, we were learning about the binding of Isaac, how God tested Abraham's faith by commanding him to sacrifice his son. Abraham prepares his donkey and takes Isaac and wood for kindling and walks to the place God has shown him. At the final moment, Isaac is saved—a ram appears, to be sacrificed in his stead. Our teacher explains that Abraham has proven he is God-fearing, that he has passed God's test. But she never explains what kind of God would ask a father to kill his child, what kind of God would ask a father to hurt his child in the first place.

"Oh, please," Eden says. She doesn't care about school nights or anything else. "She has to let you. Tell her I said so."

When Eden's mom picks us up from school, she is wearing ripped jeans and a leather jacket and has her pack of Winston Reds sitting right next to her, like she always does. I could tell she'd gone to the beauty parlor that day because, instead of her long red hair being straight and feathered on the sides, it was three times its usual size, with lots of loose waves. She'd also had her nails done, red tips with rhinestones, and I knew that later she would dance around the house, dangling her nails out in front of her, saying, "Look, I'm a movie staahhh."

My mom never gets her nails done. And she never wears jeans, ripped or otherwise. She only wears long skirts or dresses, believing pants for women are immodest.

"Look at you gorgeous girls," Eden's mom says as we climb into the car.

"Gimme a kiss," she says to Eden. "I missed you so much."

That's how Eden's mom spoke to her: like she was the most important person in the world.

Joy was the name of Eden's mom, and Joy was the only thing you could call her.

"Why would I want to be called Mrs.-the-name-of-my-first-husband?" she would say. "I divorced that son of a bitch when Eden was only one year old."

Nor did she want to be called Mrs.-the-name-of-her-second-husband, since he'd been even worse than the first. When Joy got married for the third time, Eden got to have her nails painted pink and her hair done up with baby's breath, and I thought I'd never seen anyone look so beautiful in my life.

One time when I was sleeping over, Joy told me and Eden that if she ever got pregnant again, she would have an abortion. I knew the implications of the word, if not the details. I knew also what it implied about Joy—that she was the wrong kind of mother, a selfish woman thinking only of herself, which is no kind of mother at all. In the end, she did not have an abortion. Eden now had a little baby brother named Brandon. But just because she had the baby did not mean she was happy.

At night, as we're falling asleep, I tell Eden everything. About my mom and the baby and my dad and my sister, whom I'm always fighting with. Eden listens, like she always does. She listens and listens, even when it gets late, even when she gets tired, even when she says, "My eyes are closed, but I'm still listening."

The baby is a boy, which means there's a bris, held at our house eight days after he is born. It's not my first. I already have two little brothers, and I can remember theirs distinctly. The shiny cutting instruments glinting in the morning light, the smell of smoked fish, the specter of blood. Then there were the brises of various congregants' sons that I'd attended. At the last one, I'd fainted.

My grandfather, my mother's father, has flown in from California for the occasion, arriving in his dark green Rolls Royce with a silk handkerchief in his breast pocket. A self-made businessman from Chicago's South Side, he'd never approved of my father. Why would he? My grandfather had no respect for religion, which he considered outdated—an illusion for those too weak to face life. Then there was the fact that my father did not make enough money. The congregation tried to act like they respected their rabbi so much, but when it came to paying his salary, they were always looking to cut corners. When it was time for tuition payments or car payments or summer camp, my mother always called her father.

My grandfather knew what kind of man my father was the minute he'd laid eyes on him: a man who could not be trusted. He could see that right away—something shifty, grandiose. Nobody had to explain this to me—I could feel it. Since the first time my grandfather met my father, he'd begged my mother to leave him, but she never would. Even when she admitted to her father that her husband hit her, she would not leave. What could her father do? Now he was paying for the catering—baskets of bagels, mountains of egg salad, neat rows of lox. In the center of the table was a whole poached salmon lying on its side, covered in cucumbers made to look like scales, its eye intact and staring at the ceiling.

At the time of my baby brother's bris, I was still young, but I was old enough to understand the impact my father was already having on the community. Since we moved to our tidy suburb, the Rubenfeld family had started keeping kosher, and so had the Finermans and the Wassersteins and the Schwartzes. On any given Sunday afternoon, my father could be found at his congregants' homes, explaining the two sets of dishes, the carefully separated

sets of silverware. He blowtorched their ovens and poured scald-
ing water over their sinks and countertops, extolling the virtues
of a kosher home.

Every family who took on the laws of kashrut or the strictures
of the Sabbath or who began sending their children to religious
school was another triumph for my father. He was bringing the
living waters of Torah to the people of our prosperous town, who
hadn't even realized how thirsty they were.

If you want to know what kind of rabbi my father is, he isn't
going to tell you. That's because he's the kind of rabbi who does not
believe in creating divisions, only in what brings us closer to God. In
practice, my father's religious views fell somewhere between Conservative and Orthodox, though he refused to align himself with
any denomination. He refused to pay dues to the National Council
of Synagogues, the United Synagogue of Conservative Judaism, the
National Council of Young Israel, the Orthodox Union, or anyone
else who could claim authority over his dominion.

Men and women sat together in his synagogue, yet only men
were permitted to chant from the Torah scroll. Though he personally observed the laws of the Sabbath, he allowed his congregants
to drive to synagogue, despite the halachic prohibition against it.
Decades before it was fashionable, he believed in finding com-
monality with other religious leaders, and he met regularly with
the imam from the local Islamic Cultural Center and the priest
from Our Lady of the Brook.

Many of my father's congregants had joined the synagogue
after seeing him officiate at a wedding or funeral. Moved by my
father's words, comforted by his sincerity, dazzled by a single, isolated encounter, they'd become members. Only later would they
ask what type of rabbi my father was.

"I'm a Jew," my father would answer, when pressed. "I answer only to God."

As a child, I admired his embattled faith, his refusal to submit to man-made categories. But as an adult, I would come to understand: it is easier to hold oneself accountable to God than to human beings.

Looking back, I can understand the deal the people in the suburbs had made, with their big houses and fancy cars, their two or three children. Yes, they went to Vail every winter and to Miami every spring, but somehow, something was missing. For all their monetary accomplishments, my father's congregants wanted to be reminded of where they'd come from. They wanted to hear the kiddush over the wine sung the way their *zeyde* had sung it; they wanted to eat challah made by hand; they wanted to hear Kol Nidre once a year and pound their chests and eat a bagel on an empty stomach and a clear conscience. They wanted to be able to say that the rabbi who bar mitzvahed their son was a "wonderful guy" and "also a friend." They wanted a glimpse of an authentic Torah life, the exact thing their parents or grandparents had turned away from in their pursuit to become American.

That was where my father came in, with his warm smile and white teeth, offering a taste of authenticity, an authenticity that was so missing in their lives—driving on the gray highways every weekday from their house to the office to the gym, and on the weekends from the house to the mall—that when my father said, "Come for Shabbos," they did, so honored to be invited into the sacredness of the rabbi's home.

Decades from now, when I learn the worst things a daughter can learn about a father, I will think of all the people my father brought back to God. I will think of the holiness he brought into their lives and wonder if this will help him in the heavenly court, if his good deeds will outweigh the bad.

My parents had decided to have the bris recorded, which means a videographer they brought in is walking around with a microphone and a video camera, interviewing people and videotaping the whole thing.

"You excited to be a big sister again?" he says as he shoves the microphone in my face.

No, I was not excited to be a big sister again. I pretend not to hear him and turn to walk away, but our modest split-level is so packed, there is hardly any room to move, and now my aunt and uncle are there, telling me how proud I should be of my mother.

"Now you're the oldest of five," my aunt Lily says. "That's a big responsibility."

"She's up for it," my uncle Peter says, giving me a smile.

I smile back, even though I don't feel like smiling. From upstairs, I can hear Uncle Peter and Aunt Lily's honey-haired daughter, Sloan, trying to get three-year-old Ephraim to talk to the video camera. "Don't you want to be a movie star?" she asks. As the rabbi's children, we were always expected to perform.

Unlike the congregants, I am pretty sure Uncle Peter knows what is happening in our home, but when I talk to him, he makes like he doesn't. I want to ask him how it's possible that everyone is looking at the same thing, but no one can see what's happening—how everyone can see what they want to see, but no one can see what I do. Of course, I do not ask him this, nor do I tell Aunt Lily the correct term is "eldest," which I know from my father. Whenever he introduces me to a new congregant, he puts his hands on my shoulders and says, "This is Sara, our eldest."

My grandfather serves as the sandek, holding the softly sleeping baby while the mohel prepares his tools. The baby is laid on his back in the middle of our wood-laminate kitchen table, and a wine-soaked piece of gauze is placed in his mouth.

Every time the baby cries, it makes me nervous. It is hard to see how I could be related to this wrinkled, shrieking creature. I know he will be another source of my mother's sleepless nights, another reason I don't have my own room. Still, it isn't the baby's fault he'd been born. I could feel the tears rise up behind my eyes. None of this was his fault, none of it at all.

Right before he cuts, the mohel announces the baby's name: Noam, which means pleasantness, further proof of my mother's delusion.

When I hear Noam cry, I want to cry too. I want to tell him everything is going to be okay, that no one is going to hurt him, but that would be a lie. He was going to be hurt many times, and I knew it.

It's at recess a few weeks later that my friend Anne tells me her mother's pregnant, due at the end of the summer. We are standing out in the cold by the monkey bars, all the girls huddled close to keep warm, while the boys run around the field with a football. We both know it's ridiculous for Anne's parents to have a baby, because they run a kosher catering business and all they do is work, and when they aren't working, they're arguing. It was Anne's parents who catered my brother's bris, her mother who arranged the whole fish on our table.

"Why does she think she has the right to do this?" Anne asks me.

"I have no idea," I tell her. "It's obscene."

I feel bad for Anne, but it isn't just that. There's an anger building inside me, an anger I try so hard not to let myself know I feel.

I am in the car with my mother, driving from one place to another, when I tell her about Anne's mom.

"I just don't think it's fair to Anne," I say.

"What do you mean 'fair to Anne'?"

"You know Anne's parents," I tell her. "You know how they are."

But she does not know how they are. Nor does she care. What she knows is that a baby is going to be born, and that that is a miracle.

"Every baby brings its own blessing," she tells me.

"I know," I tell her. "A gift from God."

Does she think that I don't know this? It's the Torah's first commandment, to be fruitful and multiply, to populate the earth with holy souls. That was what she would say if you asked why she kept having children. But I knew that wasn't the real reason. The real reason had nothing to do with the Torah or God or anything else. It was that my mother had grown up alone, alone in the big house after her mother died and her older brothers had moved away.

I never knew my mother's mother, only what I'd heard. There is the part about who she was, then there is the part about what happened to her body. Before she got sick, she woke up every day at noon in time for cards with her friends. Her nails were always painted a dark shade of red, her black hair always waved, a cigarette always in her hand.

My mother says her mother never loved her, never even liked her.

When she says that, her father says, "Are you kidding? You were the apple of her eye."

What my mother remembers is people telling her to be quiet. What my mother remembers is her aunt Evelyn telling her that the best present she could give her mother was to leave her alone. But the other thing she remembers is her mother screaming. Screaming in pain. She remembers going into her mother's room, and seeing her mother's back, as she was turned to the wall. Her mother tells her to go away, to go away; she doesn't want her daughter to see her in pain, to know what pain looks like. But one time she did see. "She didn't mean for me to see," my mother tells me. "She never would have wanted me to see, but I once saw her body. The whole top of it carved out, everything from the waist up gouged until there was nothing left."

I look over at my mom, her hands gripping the steering wheel, and I can see her face harden. It's easy to look at my dad and say he's the reason I feel sad, but that is only part of the story. The other part is how my mother's anger could appear fully formed out of nowhere.

"You're just selfish!" she screams at me. "You think you're God? You think you get to decide whether a child comes into this world?"

My heart is pounding. "No, of course not. What I meant is that—"

But she doesn't care what I meant. She cares only that I am selfish, selfish at my core. That I am not a generous person like she is.

"You don't love your brother?" my mother asks. "You're not happy he was born?"

My mother knows I love him, his chubby legs and huge blue eyes, and this is how she traps me.

"Of course I love Noam," I tell her. "That is not the point."

"Then what is the point?" she says.

But by then I've forgotten. Or maybe I never knew in the first place. What was my point?

That I was still angry, that I would always be angry?

Three months later, my mother takes me shopping to buy my first bra. It's not like I really need it, but Eden's been wearing one for months, and so have Anne and Deborah, and it can't be put off any longer.

When we arrive at Schwartz's Intimate Apparel, I'm amazed at the variety. You can't see most of the bras, which are kept in a bank of shallow drawers behind the counter, but this sign catches my attention: ASK US ABOUT OUR CUSTOM EXPERT FITTINGS FOR MASTECTOMY AND RECONSTRUCTIVE SURGERIES. My mom sees the sign too and stops and stares.

"You would never see a sign like that," she says to me. "There was nothing like that when my mom was sick."

The summer is coming, and soon we'll be leaving for California to visit my grandfather. Everyone except my father, who, of course, has to work, whose work never stops. "It'll be good for your father to have some time to himself," my mother says, but I know she isn't talking about my father. She is talking about herself.

The week before we leave, Eden invites herself to sleep over. Since the spring, she's been spending more time at my house. We never talk about it, but I know it's because of Joy. Lately, whenever I go over, she doesn't want to take us out for waffles or to rent movies like she used to, or even to run to the convenience store with her when she runs out of cigarettes. Some days, when we get home from school, Joy is just sitting there on the couch in

THERE WAS NIGHT AND THERE WAS MORNING   35

front of the big-screen TV, but the TV isn't on. On these nights, Don takes us out for dinner, or Eden makes us scrambled eggs or a salad with everything in it.

A storm was coming. From our front porch, where Eden and my mom and I were sitting on a Saturday afternoon, you could easily see it. The sky had turned light yellow and green, and everything was giving off its muted glow in the middle of the afternoon.

Eden could sing. Just like my mother could sing. When they opened their mouths, it didn't matter what the song was, the sound that came out was pure. I also liked to sing, but singing was not a gift I possessed, even if it was the one I wanted most.

On this day of the storm, before it actually began but just as it was picking up its eerie speed and leaking its yellow-green light everywhere, Eden and my mother sat on our porch and sang. They sang songs from *Gypsy* and *Cats* and *A Chorus Line,* and then they sang the "Star-Spangled Banner" over and over. Hours earlier, my mom had put out glass bowls filled with plums and ice on the porch. But the ice had melted, leaving the purple-black spheres swimming in water.

I looked at my mom, with her clear eyes and clear voice, and tried to freeze the moment in my mind. I thought of all the times I wished that she would ask me about my homework, or if I wanted to go shopping, or why I was so sad. I thought of all the times I tried to talk to her but she was too busy with the baby or the dishes or the laundry. She always said she loved me, but how stupid did she think I was?

I think about the last time I'd slept at Eden's, when I read her a story I'd written about a girl whose mother dies, a girl who doesn't want to go to her mother's funeral because she doesn't know what to wear. Eden loved this story so much she made me show it to Joy, and Joy loved it so much she made me call up Eden's grandmother and read it to her over the phone. Joy loved this story so much she said, "One day you'll be a famous writer. One day you'll write a story about me."

4

THE LETTER

IF A BOY TALKS ABOUT SEX, he has done nothing wrong; he has simply taken his place in the order of things. If a girl talks about sex, she's done everything wrong; a specter of suspicion hangs above her like a cloud. The thing about girls is they are daughters. And what if you're the daughter of a man selling the idea of a God-fearing family? A daughter like that must be a good daughter, and the only way to be a good daughter is to follow the rules God has prescribed to keep you that way.

I met the boy the first day of middle school, when two smaller schools joined into one. I didn't meet him right away, it's true, but I did notice him because he was my age, yet he didn't seem that way. For one thing, he had shoulders, something none of the other boys had, though he still wore the plaid shirts his mother bought him, because while the girls went to the mall on the weekends, the boys still had their mothers buying their clothes.

In social studies class, the boy stared at Jessica, who stared back. Jessica had long blond curly hair, both dyed and permed, and wore stretchy spandex jeans. There were times before gym class when I would see Jessica and the boy coming out of the girls' locker room together and days when he would look at me when no one was around and say, "Hey, wanna go to the locker room with me?" and laugh and walk away, and I didn't know what to do, so I laughed too. I tried to laugh as hard as he laughed. Jessica rarely laughed at all, and when she did, it was in a high-pitched screech divided up like hiccups.

Eden and I would spend hours talking about this boy. Eden had ideas about what he and Jessica did together when they disappeared into the locker room. Another boy liked me, and I ignored him. He would give Eden messages to give to me or questions to ask me, and I would say to Eden, "Tell me again what your mother says guys like." I wanted the boy to look at me without laughing, the way he looked at Jessica.

Sometimes the boy would tell me I laughed too much, and I knew this to be true, so I tried to be someone he could take seriously.

It is Abigail Gorenstein's bat-mitzvah party, and the music is pounding from the speakers set up in front of the DJ station. The best bar mitzvah parties had themes—Matt's was "The Fifties," Illana's was "Hawaiian Luau," Eden's was "Eden's Mall," where everyone got a chocolate credit card with their name and table number inscribed in hot-pink fondant—but Abigail's party doesn't have a theme.

The party is in the basement of a synagogue, but with the lights off and a colorful strobe emanating from the stage, it feels like a disco. The synthesizer sets the beat as a woman's voice soars above it.

The adults are still talking at their tables or milling about the dessert station. The DJ has two assistants—guys who look like maybe they're in college or at least high school—and their job is to get us dancing. It doesn't take much for me and Eden. We are always the first ones on the dance floor. We jump and spin as we mouth the words of the song, and the other girls circle around us, jumping, spinning, mouthing the words too.

The boy comes over to me while I'm hot and sweaty, and he takes my wrist and says, "C'mere, I want to talk to you." Eden looks at me and smiles, because she knows this is what I have been waiting for. I step out of my circle, and I go with the boy, who is holding me by the wrist, and he finds a door—how does he know where a door is or where it will lead to?—and the door takes us up a stairwell to another floor, a floor that is empty on a Sunday afternoon.

We are in some kind of office or classroom, and the room is dark.

"I don't think you would ever really do anything," he tells me.

"That's not true," I tell him. "I would do something."

And I would. I would do something right now. But then there is the sound of doors opening and the sound of other boys' laughter, a group of boys that goes roaming the corridors during a lull in the party's festivities, maybe as the speeches begin, looking for couples like us. They burst into the room, making loud kissing sounds. "Get out of here!" I tell them, but by the time I turn around, the boy is gone, and I wonder when I will get the chance to show him he is wrong.

My father needed a break. It was understandable, my mother said. Most men had one boss, but my father had hundreds. "Every congregant thinks they're the most important," she told me. "Your father can't win." If he spent too much time visiting Mr. Schwartz at the hospital, someone would say he should have been at the budget-planning meeting. Or else Mrs. Traubman wanted to know why the rabbi had managed to visit Mr. Schwartz, but not her late mother when she was hospitalized two years ago with kidney failure. He needed to get away, to go somewhere where he was not the rabbi.

My father's mother, whom we called Nana, offered a solution: he should come to stay with her in Manhattan. A few days in the city, being back on the East Coast for even a short time—she knew it would restore him. It was her idea too that I accompany him. I was the eldest, after all; my bat mitzvah was coming up in the spring.

And so it was arranged: My father and I would leave on a Saturday night, after the Sabbath was over, after havdalah, the ceremony that marks the division between sacred and ordinary time. On the airplane, my father took off the yarmulke he usually wore and replaced it with a cap. Instead of a suit, he wore corduroys. When the stewardesses came by with their carts and asked what type of beverage we wanted, my father asked for a tomato juice with a wedge of lemon and a packet of salt and pepper, so I did too.

The truth was he'd been pretty good lately. He was trying. I had to give him credit for that.

This wouldn't be my first visit to New York. The last time, my dad took my sister and me, and we ate warm corned beef sandwiches at the kind of restaurant where the waiters wore tuxedos and said, "By all means" whenever you asked for something. My sister and I tried, but we couldn't stop laughing. Soon our dad was saying this in response to everything.

"Can you pass the ketchup?"

"By all means!"

"Can we order dessert?"

"By all means!"

When the waiter came by again, we ordered ice cream, even though it was a kosher restaurant, which meant the ice cream was fake, and the waiter said, "By all means," which got us going all over again. At home, there were only three kosher restaurants—the pizza place, the other pizza place, and the Chinese takeout—which means we hardly ever went out to eat at all. But in New York, things were different in every way.

That night, the three of us got dressed up and took a taxi-cab to the Winter Garden Theatre. My grandmother had gotten us tickets, like she always did. Our seats were fourth-row center, which, she explained, were the best in the house.

"Those are Betty Buckley's seats," she informed us, "but I told Betty that my gorgeous dolls are coming all the way from Chicago, and she insisted you have them, my darlings."

Betty Buckley was the star of the show, and my grandmother knew her personally, or at least she said she did, given that my grandmother had worked in the show's accounting department for years.

It was hard for me to understand what the play was supposed to be about. "A play just about cats?" I'd asked Nana. "It doesn't make sense."

But sitting there in Betty Buckley's seats, I changed my mind. For one thing, the actors weren't cats; they were humans made to look like cats, and as they sang, they danced and jumped and prowled against the night sky, then made their way through the audience, coming so close you could see the painted whiskers on their faces. During the final scene, when Old Deuteronomy escorts Grizabella to the Heaviside Layer, I looked over at my father, his face a silhouette in the darkened theater, and I knew that he would understand, maybe better than anyone, what I was feeling right then, the same feeling I had when I was little and he used to tell me about how God created the universe.

This trip, we weren't seeing a play. Instead, Auntie Sonia was coming in from New Jersey to spend the day taking us to galleries in a place called Soho. Auntie Sonia was my father's older sister and was unlike any other woman I knew. For one thing, she had a job. She was an interior decorator, and she drove around with books of fabric and wallpaper swatches in the back of her car. She drank coffee in the mornings and cocktails in the evenings and wore fitted skirts and high heels and painted her nails burgundy, all of which made her the opposite of my mother, and exactly the kind of woman I wanted to be.

My father and I take a taxi from the airport to my grandmother's fourth-floor apartment, not far from Central Park. She has been on her own since her husband died, whereupon she left Florida and moved back to New York City to get her CPA. As she herself has explained to me many times, she is only able to live where she does because of rent control, just one of the many magical things about the city. She never spoke of her husband—my father's father—nor did anyone else.

When we arrive, dinner is already waiting, laid out on a small glass table in the main room.

"My dolls! My beautiful dolls!" she cries when she sees us.

"Look at this gorgeous doll!" she demands, and holds me so close I can smell the Opium perfume radiating off her skin, the perspiration between her breasts.

Aside from the bedroom and the bathroom, the apartment has only one room, but it is the best room you've ever seen—an entire wall packed floor to ceiling with the paintings she and her husband had once collected and displayed at their house in Miami, the paintings my father had grown up with, before his father lost all his money and died and most of the paintings were sold. In one corner stands an antique piano stacked with sheet music from the 1930s. In another corner, a mirrored vanity displays photographs in mirrored frames. A massive wooden bureau contains a drop-desk with a mirrored bar, a stack of cocktail napkins, and a tumbler full of swizzle sticks.

"What can I get you to drink, my doll?" she asks my father.

"I'm fine, Mother," he says.

"Oh, c'mon, darling . . . after a flight, you need a drink. Let me make you something."

"I said I'm fine, Mother," he says and goes into the bathroom and shuts the door.

That was always how he spoke to her—like he was angry at her, though for the life of me, I couldn't figure out why. She was always talking about his accomplishments, how brilliant he was, like when he won the debate championship his senior year of high school. "Not the local championship," she'd remind us, "the *national* championship. Your father had to fly all the way from Miami to Omaha." After that, he was offered a scholarship to Dartmouth—"a *full* scholarship," she'd remind us, but by then he was tired of debating. He didn't want to argue anymore.

After dinner, my dad pushes the glass table into the corner and unfolds the sofa bed. My grandmother makes it up for him with sheets and fresh pillowcases, and I change into my pajamas and climb into bed with my grandmother, who is watching her small black-and-white television. "It's ten o'clock, do you know where your children are?" the newscaster asks.

"*I* know," she says, and gives me a wink.

"Is your dad sleeping?" she asks.

"I think so."

She turns off the TV, and it makes a soft, sputtering sound before the picture dies. We can both hear my father snoring in the next room.

"Listen, my darling, I want to let you know that I know it's not always easy with your dad."

I knew she knew what was happening in our home, because sometimes at night I could hear my mother speaking to her on the phone. My grandmother pauses, studies my face for a reaction.

"But you have to know how much he loves you, darling. It's always, 'Sara this, Sara that.' He just adores you. You must know that."

I get the hot feeling on my face and then the twirling in my stomach. For a minute, I think I will be quiet. But then there are words coming out of my mouth.

"He doesn't act like it," I tell her. "You don't know what it's like."

"Maybe not, darling. But here's what I do know. I know your father has a tremendous amount of pressure on him. He has to deal with that idiot, the new president of the board . . . what's his name? The one who doesn't appreciate him at all?"

"Fiegelson," I say.

"Yes, darling, Fiegelson. Can you imagine being belittled by these fools—by Fiegelson and who's the other one?"

"Bloom," I say.

"Yes, Bloom. You don't know how alone your dad feels. He needs you. He needs your support, your respect. It means everything to him."

She lowers her voice. "And I'm not sure that your mother, as amazing as we all know she is, can fully grasp what he's going through."

"What do you mean?" I ask.

"You know how I feel about your mother, darling—I love her as much as my own daughters. Oh, I felt so lucky when Danny brought her home to me! She had just gotten back from her travels—she was so tan, so beautiful, I loved her right away. Anyone would! But you know"—and here she lowered her voice further—"she doesn't have your sensitivity, my darling. You're the eldest. You understand your dad in a way no one else can."

The next morning, Auntie Sonia arrives from Montclair.

"Wait till you see this new artist I've discovered," she tells me. "He's doing completely new things with plastic."

After the galleries, we go to the Lower East Side to eat at a kosher Japanese restaurant, where my father and Auntie Sonia order actual raw fish. My father's old friend Shimon joins us— Shimon and his beautiful wife, Shoshana, who now live in Queens—and my dad and Shimon talk about what it was like when they were studying in Jerusalem, before they had to think about their building funds or dealing with their boards or paying for Jewish day school.

While they talk, Auntie Sonia asks me questions. She wants to know what kind of music I listen to, who my favorite artist is. After lunch, there's a store she wants to take us to, a gigantic warehouse with stacks of jeans going up to the ceiling, floating racks of sparkly things; you can't tell if they're shirts or dresses or what. Auntie Sonia walks around like a detective, examining random items as though for clues; she keeps talking about someone named Betsey Johnson. My dad says he's tired, he's going to find a place to sit. But first he says to me, "Why don't you try some stuff on? I'll buy you whatever you want."

When I get back from New York, the boy can tell I'm different. The reason I know is that he starts to call me on the phone. Some nights he calls, and if I say can I call you back, because I'm about to eat dinner with my family or I'm about to go grocery shopping with my mom, he says no. This boy is very smart, and I always want to get to that part of him, the part of him that writes essays that our teacher says are "an example for all of you" when she reads his work aloud in class.

Everyone should express themselves as clearly as this boy does, I agree. I cannot help but agree, because I also want to express myself. I also want to say what I want. I also want to get what I want when I ask for it. I want to express to him that I'm smart too. I'm smart like him, and I want to ask him why he doesn't know that.

Sometimes when he calls, he reads to me from a magazine. I don't know where he gets this magazine. He reads me a story from the magazine. The story is about a man and his secretary. The man is the woman's boss, but the woman also has plenty to say. The man tells the woman to lie down on the man's desk. The woman does it. The woman tells the man what she wants him to do. The man does it. The woman says do it faster, do it again, don't stop. The boy reads me this story while I am sitting at my desk in the room I share with my sister, with my math homework spread out in front of me. The boy says, "I want you to talk to me like that." I ask, "Like what?" He says, "What do you think? Like the woman in the story."

I try to say some of the words the woman in the story has said. I imagine what some of them mean. He says, "Don't just say what I just read to you. Can't you think of your own things to say?" This makes me think for the first time that he thinks I'm smart. In English class, Mrs. Potok says, "Look how clearly he conveys his ideas, how he doesn't complicate the paragraph with information that is irrelevant to the topic sentence." This is something I am often found guilty of doing. I am always giving irrelevant information—"padding," Mrs. Potok calls it—mostly because I like the way the words feel. I think they're pretty and gentle, and I don't want to cast them off.

Soon the boy tires of this game, and he asks me to write him a letter. I know better now than to ask what kind of letter it is that he wants, because by this time I know exactly. I do not need to imagine what it is the boy wants from me. He has made it crystal clear.

The part I cannot imagine is that, by writing this letter, I will make myself into a moving target. The part I cannot imagine is how this letter will ensure that the question is no longer whether I'll be punished, only when and in what form.

I begin the letter "Dear," and I put in the boy's name. Then I write about the things I want to do to him. They are the things he has told me I want to do to him, things the woman in the story wants to do to her boss.

I write this letter with a blue Paper Mate ballpoint pen on a piece of notebook paper torn from my social studies notebook. I write neatly. I have always been proud of my handwriting. It is one of the things about myself that I have always been most proud of.

You need to know the details so you can understand how they will be used against me.

I write drafts of this letter—a first draft, a second draft, a third draft, a fourth draft—shredding each one into pieces before wrapping them up in paper towels and burying them in the trash can in the kitchen. I use the words I know the boy wants to hear; I write about the things I know he wants me to write about, but I make them my own. I want to show him I am smarter than he thinks I am, that he will get more from me than he thought he would.

5

GIRLS WHO AREN'T PRAYING

WHEN I GRADUATE FROM MIDDLE SCHOOL, there's a party. A party in a synagogue basement, and I've been planning my outfit for weeks. The short black skirt I bought with Auntie Sonia when I visited her in New Jersey, a white T-shirt tucked in, dangly silver earrings mixing with my hair. Eden's wearing eyeliner, and so am I. I'm almost fourteen now.

At the party, there are teachers upstairs, but they don't come down. The boy is there, but he's not the point. I am there to dance with Eden, to remember all the things sliding into the past. But when the boy grabs my hand, when he finds an empty stairwell, I follow him, of course I follow him, because this is still my dream.

I am no longer a child, so when he kisses me, I kiss back. Even when he brings my hand to his zipper, I kiss back.

"Do you feel what you're doing to me?" he asks, and in that moment, I know I have all the power.

When I get home, I look at myself in the mirror, my face aglow, my eyes wide open. Tomorrow, I will call Eden and review every detail. I know I'm supposed to feel bad because touching a boy the way I touched this boy is not something a rabbi's daughter should be doing, but what I feel instead is proud. I know something I didn't know before, something about how the world works, the underlying thrum that animates everything.

When I graduate from middle school, there are two choices: the local public high school or the Jewish Academy, the only Modern Orthodox high school in the city of Chicago. The local public high school offers an education of the highest quality, and things a small Orthodox high school cannot—a theater department, a student newspaper, a literary magazine. A handful of kids from my class will be attending the Academy in the fall, but most will go to public school. I imagine doing things I've seen girls on TV do: trying out for a play, posing for a prom picture.

My parents both agree I should go to the Academy, but of the two, my father is more reasonable. He understands the opportunities offered by a well-funded public school. The same cannot be said of my mother, whose ideas about religion have slowly become more extreme, as though faith were a contest only the most stringent could win. Following the advice of a radio talk-show host she'd begun listening to, my mother informs me that she would send me to Catholic school before she'd send any child of hers to public school. At least at Catholic school they believe in God, she says. Going to public school means doing drugs. It means having sex. It means forgetting who you are.

"It's the first step toward assimilation," my mother tells me in the car on the way from one place to another. "It's the beginning of the decay of Judaism."

I don't want Judaism to decay, and I don't want to assimilate. But I've heard about the rules at the Academy, the ones about how boys and girls cannot touch, how prom is prohibited, how everyone has to stand when a rabbi enters the room. I've heard the rumors, whispered on the bus, told third- and fourth-hand, about the girl who got suspended for giving a boy a high five in the hallway.

There was also the matter of the dress code. Boys were required to wear a small cloth skullcap to show they were God-fearing. Girls were required to wear long skirts to show they were modest. The skirts were required to cover girls' knees, their sleeves to reach no less than halfway between the shoulder and elbow.

When I toured the school the previous spring, I couldn't help but notice the girls' faces—the bloat, the puffiness—like they weren't getting enough oxygen or were eating too much bread. In fact, there was a joke:

QUESTION: *What do you call a pretty girl at the Academy?*
ANSWER: *A visitor.*

There were no trees, no fields, no benches, no campus of any kind. No extracurriculars aside from basketball and yearbook. Just ten hours a day of school, followed by three hours a night of homework.

"If I go to the Academy, I'm going to be fat and ugly and miserable," I tell Eden.

"That's impossible," Eden says, and for the first time, I think she may be wrong.

I cry and I bargain, but it makes no difference. My parents, united in a cause, have made their decision.

At the Academy, our days are cleaved into two. Holy subjects in the morning—Bible, Prophets, Hebrew language, Jewish law. Unholy subjects in the afternoon—English, math, biology, American history, Western civilization. The school is located in West Rogers Park, a middle-class neighborhood on the far north side of the city, in the heart of Chicago's religious Jewish community.

I live far from this school, situated near the kosher pizza parlors, the ultra-Orthodox synagogues, the Judaica shops on Devon Avenue. Although I have spent my whole life living by the Torah's rules, this will be my first time being around others like me.

In order to arrive at school in time for morning prayers, I have to leave my house at seven; the school day is long, incorporating all that is holy and not holy, and I return home at seven in the evening. When the winter comes, I will leave in the dark and return in the dark. As though I have no need for sunlight.

There's no sanctuary at the Academy, just a highly waxed gym floor, covered with a green tarp to prevent the scratches from 350 folding chairs, where prayers are held every morning. I sit in a row with my new friends—Esti and Shayna and Batsheva, girls whose every action reminds me they are not Eden. We go together to the bathroom to look at ourselves in the mirror, and they even laugh at my jokes, but the most necessary element is missing.

Most of what I would come to understand about Chicago's religious Jewish community I would only understand in retrospect. Like all religious communities, the Jewish community runs on money. It's the rich who fund the city's yeshivas and girls' schools, its synagogues, study halls, sanctuaries, and ritual baths, the rich whose names appear in the annual ad books and who sit on the boards.

The community loved to honor their benefactors, praising their selflessness and generosity and their devotion to Jewish education, though no one liked to look too closely at where the money came from. When words like "bribery" or "kickback scheme" appear from time to time in connection with some of the city's most important religious families, nobody says a word. Even decades later, when the scion of one of Chicago's most charitable families is found guilty of one of the greatest fraud cases in American history, the city's yeshivas and religious schools continue to proudly bear his name.

It's still the beginning of the year, just a few weeks after the High Holidays. Outside, the scent of fall lingers just long enough to warn of the frigid Midwestern winter that's coming. Inside, Giveret Orenberg, who teaches Honors Hebrew, is patrolling the gym floor. She is looking for girls who aren't praying.

Of the *limudei kodesh* teachers, Giveret Orenberg is the only one who does not cover her hair with a wig or a scarf, as the Torah commands. Instead, she dyes her hair jet-black and pulls it into a viselike bun. She is not American, and she wears high-heeled boots and a series of silver bracelets snaking up her right arm. On her other arm, she keeps a rumpled Kleenex tucked into her sleeve.

She looks at me with a fish's cold, milky eyes. Her skin is parched, and I can see patches of scalp where her hair's been pulled thin. She taps a finger to her prayer book.

"*Lamah at lo mitpalelet?*" she demands.

She wants to know why I am not praying.

The question has multiple answers, but I know she is not interested in answers, only in compliance. Nor can I point out the obvious: that if she is focused on whether or not I am praying, how can she be praying herself? I want to ask if she thinks I am obligated in a way she is not, but we both know the truth: as females, neither of us is obligated.

Prayer is different for boys. They have to tie themselves up with leather the length of their forearms and affix small leather boxes to their heads. They have to take the Torah scroll out of the ark, undress it, and read it aloud. When they are done reading, they hold the scroll up for everyone to see—even the girls across the partition—then place it back in a small wooden closet until they read it again several days later.

As girls, we do none of this. We just watch.

This is not the only way in which life at the Academy is different for girls, whose modesty is the school's utmost concern. According to the dress code, the hem of a girl's skirt is required to cover her knees—not to hover *near* her knees or *above* her knees, but to obscure them completely. Naturally, it fell to the vice principal, Rabbi Nussbaum, to enforce this rule, which he did by eyeballing girls' hems as he strolled the hallways. If a girl's skirt was too short, she was called into the office or sent home with a suspension.

Why is it a grown man's business what a teenage girl is wearing?

Why is it his job to measure the length of her skirt?

Why, if the purpose of the dress code is to protect a girl's modesty, is he looking at her at all?

I do not yet have the words to explain why this is wrong, but that doesn't mean the words aren't growing inside me.

Giveret Orenberg taps a finger to her prayer book again. She is looking at me with her fish's eyes, waiting for an answer. I am not stupid. I understand she is the teacher and I am the student. I understand she is the type of person who needs to control people in order to feel alive. I understand that she has all the power and I have none. There's only one way to play this game. I look down at my prayer book and pretend to pray.

We do not study with the boys, at least not the holy subjects, but we see them in the hallways. We pass them after prayers, on the way to the cafeteria, coming out of the library. They are there, hanging around the school gym during Saturday-night basketball games. In some ways, they are so far away, but in other ways they are just close enough.

There's one boy I notice; there is always one boy I notice.

This boy has brown curly hair that he has the nerve to wear to his collar, unlike other boys with curly hair who buzz it short. He is a senior, which means he's never talked to me, but I have seen him talking to other people, really slow in his crackly voice, his small brown eyes peering out from behind wire-rimmed glasses.

He's not like the other boys, the boys who take their Talmud study seriously, the boys who leap quickly to their feet when a rabbi enters the room. No, this is a boy who wears broken-in Levi's from thrift shops on the North Side of the city, a boy who dates girls from out of town, a boy who is busy applying to small colleges in New England no one in your school has heard of. Whatever this boy wants, he can have.

I know things about this boy because I am friends with his sister, and also with a girl he used to go out with. She is beautiful in the way of girls who don't try, who brush a piece of golden hair across their forehead and a boy remembers it forever. One time, we all went swimming, and she wore a green-and-light-green-striped bikini, and I wore a modest navy one-piece with shorts, and I lay there and watched them in the sunlight like I was invisible.

One day, I see the boy in the hallway, and he is wearing a navy-blue suit and a yellow tie with blue polka dots, like a boy at a New England prep school or a boy in a picture of a catalog selling clothes to people who wish they went to a New England prep school. And this sight is so preposterous, so jarring against the backdrop of all the other mushy, mealy faces, for whom the parameters of this concrete building are all they can imagine, that as he passes, just as he crosses the threshold of my vision, I say, "Why are you wearing that?"

The boy stops, a slow smile forming on his lips, his teeth tiny stones.

"It's Rosh Chodesh," he says. The first day of the Jewish month.

Of course I know it's Rosh Chodesh—that morning, prayers took twenty-five minutes longer than usual. Rosh Chodesh celebrates the first day of the new moon, when it's just a crescent of a crescent, barely even formed. When I was young, my father explained to me about the lunar calendar that the Jewish people follow—the waxing and waning, the endless cycle of renewal, all ordained by God. On Rosh Chodesh, Hallel is recited, a series of psalms extolling God's greatness, each with its own separate melody. Since I was young, Hallel had always been my favorite prayer or series of prayers, the singing of it but also the words, especially Psalm 114:

> *What bothers you, sea, that you toss?*
>
> *The Jordan, that you run backward?*
>
> *The mountains dance like rams, the hills like young lambs.*
>
> *The whole earth trembles before the Lord, before the God*
> *   of Jacob,*
>
> *Who turns rock into a lake of water.*
>
> *Flint into a wellspring.*

At school, they call these words prayer, but I know they are poetry.

I look at the boy and wonder if he has dressed up to recite these words, to honor the holiness of the day. If it's true, it would be surprising; this boy is not known for his devotion.

"So you got dressed up for Rosh Chodesh?" I ask, and he laughs without opening his mouth.

"Yeah, Rabbi Englander gives us extra credit," he says, and again there is the smile, but just the slow crack of it, before he walks away.

I can feel the blossoming of heat on my face, the shame that for a moment I'd wondered if he'd actually dressed up of his own volition, to honor the holiness of a day. Now I see how that could never happen, how the boy isn't thinking like that. He is thinking of just one thing: the world outside these walls and how he will succeed in it.

One morning, I wake up from sleep and rub my eyes. It's still dark out: it's only 6:15, and I have to leave for school in an hour. I stumble to the shower, incapable of thinking, still half in a dream. For months now, the shower in the hallway bathroom, which I share with my sister and brothers, has been broken, or maybe it has always been broken, but now I can't deal with it anymore—the trickling pressure, the water that never fully heats up. So my mom says I can use her bathroom—that is, the one she shares with my father, the one you can reach only by walking through their bedroom.

On this morning, unlike other mornings, the door to the bedroom is locked. And if the bedroom is locked, I cannot take a shower, and I need to take a shower because I am too young to drink coffee, and the cool water rushing over my head is the only thing that can wake me up so early in the morning, and so I knock gently, aware of how early it still is. I wait at the door. I think about knocking again.

But then I hear my father. He is screaming from inside the room, and the thing he is screaming is, "*Drop dead!*"

At first, I don't know who he is talking to, and then I realize that he is talking to me.

Does your father want you to die? You're still tired, still halfway in a dream, so maybe you misheard.

"What?" I say in a regular voice, to show that I'm not angry.

But there is no response. And now I know how stupid I am, thinking he would answer me.

I go downstairs, where my mom is in the kitchen making my little brothers' lunches, the open jars of natural peanut butter and all-fruit jam in front of her. She's already been up for hours.

"Did you hear what he said? Did you hear him? He told me to drop dead! Mom!"

But my mom just shakes her head. "He's a sick man," she says. "You can't let him upset you."

"No!" I say. "I can't. I can't stand to be talked to that way."

And then my mother says what she always says.

"Don't overdramatize," she says, to remind me that I'm crazy.

That night, after I've finished my homework, but before I wash my face and go to sleep, my dad comes into my bedroom to apologize. It was all a misunderstanding.

"I'm sorry," he says. "I thought you were your mother."

I'm too old for my mother to make my lunches, so I buy them at the cafeteria. A Saran-Wrapped bagel, cream cheese spread so thick it oozes out of the hole. A premade peanut butter and jelly sandwich, neon jelly seeping through the white bread.

The problem with these meals is they never fill me up. By the time ninth period rolls around, which Esti and I both have free, we walk to the Quick-Stop down the street. There is a nice Indian man at the counter who calls us by our names, and we can buy anything we want.

We are hungry. Some days we get ice-cream sandwiches. Some days we get frozen bagel dogs, which the man at the counter heats up for us in his personal microwave, and we eat in the back of the store on the floor in front of the small frozen-foods section.

But, on this day, Esti and I buy a box of Entenmann's cinnamon rolls and two bottles of fruit punch, and because it is almost spring, we sit on a bench at the bus stop and eat them. There are six buns, enough for a family, but between the two of us, we finish the box.

"We're really pigging out," Esti says, still chewing.

"It's a pig-out party," I say.

There's nothing else for us to do.

It's because I'm friends with his sister and with the girl he used to go out with that I start going over to the boy's house. Normally, my friends' houses had plush wall-to-wall carpeting, pillows on the couches that matched the wallpaper, etc. But in this boy's house, there's no carpet anywhere, not even in the bedrooms. Just huge windows everywhere, where the light floods in during the day and the black starlessness comes in at night.

This boy loves music, and sometimes he says, "Hey, you guys wanna listen to something?" And his sister and I go into his room with its bare floors, and he plays Van Morrison, Pink Floyd, the Cowboy Junkies, even early Elton John. I do not know anything about this music before him, before he introduces me to it.

He lends me his tapes. He starts to call me, now that it is almost summer, and I sit on the couch in the living room and open the window behind me so that the wind blows on my legs while we talk. I don't know what we talk about, and it doesn't matter. I mostly listen. I listen while he tells me about what he ate for dinner or a book he just read or what happened in English class that day, and I just keep listening to every word that drips out of his slow-moving lips, and when I get off the phone, I go to sleep, and my bed suddenly feels so comfortable and everything lies right—the sheets and pillows and blanket—and nothing feels annoying, not even my sister breathing in the bed across from mine.

Because my sister and I share a room, I listen to the boy's tapes on my Walkman. This boy holds me close every night, his tiny dancer. And I'm sure that no one at school knows we talk on the phone every night because he calls me; *he calls me.* Sometimes he waits around for me outside a classroom, and I look at all the mushy mealy faces looking back at me.

One day he comes over, and we sit in my backyard after school until it gets dark, and I know this would never happen if it wasn't almost summer. Because by then I'm wearing the black T-shirt and the faded green shorts I change into as soon as I get home from school, and I put some of my hair up in a gold barrette. I don't know what we talk about that day, and it doesn't matter.

Then there's a night, maybe it is this night, when I find myself lying on his bed. I came to be lying there because I said I wasn't feeling well, and maybe I wasn't, and he came to lie next to me to see how I was. Beneath the big window, the night's coming in, and the music asks one question over and over.

The boy gets off the bed and goes to the wall and turns off the light, but not the music; that keeps going. He lies back down next to me and says how are you feeling now? and I say fine, and he says how about now? and I say fine, and he asks again, and I say nothing, and then he turns my face to his, and he says are we thinking the same thing, and I want to tell him that I am not thinking about anything, anything at all, because my mind has shredded itself up and I have set fire to the trash of it left in a heap. I'm shocked when the boy uses my name, when he calls me back from the fire with this name, as though it were a secret name or a holy name. When he uses my name, then, I feel he is calling me by a secret or bringing me into holiness, into sanctuary, into *our* sanctuary, because how could this boy know my name when I've never told him what it feels like to be thrown against a wall—*splat!*; what it feels like to see my father make homemade cornbread one night, and no one wants to eat it for some reason, and you see it sitting there, in the same place, on the same paper-towel-lined plate with the blue rim for days, the sweet oil leaving its indelible mark until my mother finally throws it away, stacked as is, in a small pyramid of neatly cut squares; what it feels like to lock myself in the downstairs bathroom and pull myself into a ball and rock back and forth on the cold black tile floor and stare at the peeling sunflower wallpaper—all these things. This boy uses my name for what feels like the first time ever, except that he must have used it; he must have used it, I think, when he used to call my house every night last spring; he must have used it to ask my mother if I was there. Was I there?

Now I must answer him; here he is, face to me now, and I must answer his question: Are we thinking the same thing?

I don't know. You tell me, I want to say. *How about I tell you what I'm thinking, and you tell me if that's what you're thinking too, because the truth is you don't know what I'm thinking.*

So I let the boy put his hand behind my neck and pull my face into his, and I let him put his tongue in my mouth and then his mouth on my neck. And I let myself go under as he goes over me. And I let myself sink down as he is moving on top. And then he takes off his glasses and puts them on a little table next to his bed, next to the book he'd been telling me about a couple days before.

The song has ended now, and so has the tape, and we both hear the final click of the empty space running out. Now there is just the silence of all the dark coming in through the window, except for his breathing, which keeps getting louder and more broken. I think of his mother, with her faraway accent, and I think how much he is like that now too, speaking in some faraway accent, in a different language entirely. I see my sweatshirt get pulled over my head; I see it go to the floor. For a little while, I open my eyes, and I don't know what I see. The boy without his glasses, he is a different person. I think I will never recognize him in school after this; he is a stranger like any other.

I'm wearing loose jeans, so there's room for his hands to go in without taking them off. I keep trying to look at his face for a sign of something. I don't know what kind of sign I am looking for, but I never see it. He is not looking for any kind of sign from me; he is not asking me any questions now.

I think this boy is a stranger, and I am right. He is a stranger at school that Monday, that Tuesday, that Wednesday, passing me nonchalantly in the hallway, enclosed in his large group of friends, so eager and thankful to be with him. He offers me a passing wave, a half smile, a delicately constructed smile with only some of his small white teeth.

Something is growing inside of me, something angry. I can tell because I cannot keep it in. It's bursting out of me, making itself known. The sudden scattering of bumps across my cheeks, the raised, red welts. My face advertises what I do not. It gives me away.

I try to pretend I'm still like my friends, still normal and happy, the way I know I should be, but I am no longer like them, if I ever was. Their skin is smooth, their faces blameless, so that even as I walk to class with them and sit next to them during prayers, we are not in the same universe. I am occupying another planet completely.

The spring catalogs come in the mail, one after the other, sometimes in duplicates. The same catalogs the boy orders his clothes from, the catalogs people who live in New England order their clothes from, the people he wants to be like.

I try everything—pink toners and blue astringents, thick beige creams in small tubes, but they do nothing. My mom makes an appointment with a dermatologist, a middle-aged woman who inspects my face with a bright light, like I'm a criminal.

"It's not just closed pustules we have here; there is also a proliferation of open pustules," the doctor says, addressing my mother.

Her recommendation is an aggressive regimen of oral antibiotics, a high-potency benzoyl peroxide cream to be applied nightly, but never during daylight, as that could burn the skin—and a series of manual extractions. The antibiotics would have to be picked up at the pharmacy, the topical cream purchased at the checkout desk, but the manual extractions would begin immediately. She does not look at me at all.

I look up at this woman, who is not looking at me, and her skin is perfect, without wrinkles or blemishes or scars of any kind, and I think I would do anything to be like her, to be that lucky. In her hand, she holds a small metal instrument, something delicate and shiny, like tweezers with a tiny hole at the tip, which she promptly begins pressing into my face without warning or explanation, so hard that tears spring to my eyes, but I will not let myself cry.

It's not that I have one or two pimples that need to be extracted. What I have is a whole face full of pores, each clogged with the accumulation of bacteria and sadness. And it is this that the dermatologist must be fighting against as she presses the extractor deep into my cheek, pressing harder and harder until she reveals a small spooling thread of sebum. But it's more than that; she is an exorcist tasked with removing the poison from my body.

When it's finally over, my skin is on fire. I have the feeling of being purified, but also of being brutalized. Not that I have those words; I am only fifteen, but I still have the feeling.

I am not crying—I promised myself I wouldn't—but my face is weeping just the same. The doctor hands me a Kleenex, which I press to my skin. It comes back spotted, the blood seeping out of me without my permission. I ask my mom if I have to go to school, and she says, "No, it's okay, you don't have to if you don't want to."

When I get home, I look at myself in the mirror. I am not expecting anything good. I can feel the open sores, the blood just beginning to clot. But nothing prepares me for what I see when I look in the mirror. I am no longer the girl I once was. I've become something else entirely.

6

YOU COULD LEARN A THING OR TWO FROM YOUR DAUGHTER

WHEN I TURN SEVENTEEN, I go out for dinner with my friends. Somewhere there's a picture: Esti and Shayna and Batsheva and I, arms linked, standing at the entrance to a nonkosher restaurant. In the picture, I am wearing a purple turtleneck dress and smiling so big.

Seventeen like the magazine, seventeen like the songs. It's the number I've been waiting for, the one that changes everything. I will follow my plan and apply for early decision to college, to the one I've been working so hard to get into, the one I got such glowing recommendations for, the one in a different state that I will fly to and never come back.

When I turn seventeen, I'm appointed editor in chief of the yearbook. Well, not really the chief, since the position's divided into three, but I'm the chief copyeditor, which means I'm in charge of the words. One of the editors is a boy named Stanislov. He was born in Russia, but came to America when he was ten. The other editor is the boy from middle school, the boy who read me stories over the phone, the stories from the magazine, the boy who asked me to write him a letter.

I did write the letter but I never gave it to him, because when the boy came over one Saturday afternoon to get it, I could not find it. I'd hidden it in the back of my closet behind my heavy winter sweaters, but when I went to retrieve it, it was gone. Because I could not find it, I thought maybe I'd imagined it. Maybe the letter had never existed.

By the time we are seniors, I've forgotten all of this, and so has the boy. Anyway, he's changed. By the time the other boys have caught up, he isn't so good-looking anymore, and he isn't even that tall.

It is night, and I am at a yearbook meeting. I am sitting at a table discussing something with Stanislov, but I can't remember what. The room is filled with people, though it's after 9:00 p.m. People have pencils in their hands and graph paper, tracing the outlines of photographs. There is the pounding rhythm of basketball practice in the gym beneath us—the echoes and shouts, the bad acoustics, the boys running fast.

There are empty pizza boxes and empty Coke cans. There's a slice of mushroom and green pepper left in one box.

I am sitting talking with Stanislov, but soon Stanislov looks up and points to the door to show me someone is here to see me. I go to the door and walk out into the hallway. It is Esti—her eyes red, her face puffy, her car keys in her hand. I am worried something's happened to her. Why else would she be here?

Esti looks at me and starts to cry. She tells me she is sorry to bother me at the yearbook meeting, but she thought I'd want to know. She tells me she thought I'd want to know right away, that as soon as she found out, she got in her car to tell me that Joy is dead, that Eden's mom has killed herself.

My mother takes me to the funeral. When I walk into the synagogue, it is already filled with people, but Eden instantly appears out of the crowd, like a ghost. She takes my hand and says, "I've been waiting for you to come."

With each passing year, Eden and I had grown further apart. Since Joy left Don, she and Eden had been living in a series of semi-furnished condos near the mall. With every move, their phone number had changed. The last time I called, the phone just rang until a voice said the number had been disconnected.

Now I follow Eden, who is leading me by the hand at her mother's funeral.

Somehow Eden is calm. She is radiant. She is wearing a black tent dress that hides her, that envelopes her, that whisks her away. She wears no makeup, just small silver earrings, her nails filed into ovals, painted pale pink. Her hair is short—she'd cut it last year—and there are wisps of it in her face. She holds my hand and doesn't let go.

Eden takes her place in the front row next to her grandmother, who sits next to her grandfather, who sits next to Don. I take my place next to Eden. Her boyfriend sits behind us with her best friends from high school.

Eden and I sit with our fingers interlaced; we do not speak. We stare straight ahead as the service begins. We hold on tight.

As they carry the casket out of the room, Eden's grandmother kisses two fingers, places them on the gleaming wood surface, and says, "Goodbye, Joy." Eden stands silently. She does not move.

After the service, I am lost. People get into their cars to drive to the cemetery, where Joy's body will be lowered into the ground forever, never to come back out. Eden lets go of my hand, follows her grandparents out of the room. My mother finds me and takes me to the car. I ask if we can go to the cemetery, but she says that we will go home.

We drive the whole way in silence. It is cold and still outside, and sunny. I think: What about the imperative to accompany the dead? To escort their souls from this world to the next? What about the commandment to bring comfort to the living?

When we get home, it's the middle of the afternoon. It's a school day, but I am not in school. When we get home, there's a message on the answering machine. It's from Jed, who was my boyfriend before he went away to college. He was different from the first boy or the second boy; he was kinder, and taller too.

It's the middle of the afternoon, and I sit in my family's living room and pick up the phone. I dial Jed's number, and he answers. It's the middle of December, and he is home for vacation. He says, "What are you doing tonight?" I say, "Nothing." He says, "Do you want to go to a movie?" And I say, "Sure."

A dark, sinking feeling falls over me, or maybe I fall into it. It's the day of Eden's mother's funeral, and for some reason I cannot understand, I am not with her, I am somewhere else—alone in the house with my mother, while my father is at work and my brothers and sister are at school.

I hang up the phone. I take off my shoes. I peel off my tights. I take off my long denim skirt. I leave these in a crumpled pile on the stained living-room carpet and walk upstairs in my bra and underwear. I go into the bathroom and turn on the hot water and let it run out of the bathtub faucet until it is very hot. Then I lift the knob that will make it come out of the showerhead. I unhook my bra and slide the wide straps off my shoulders. I pull my underwear down. I slide open the glass door and step under the stream of water and stand there for a long time. I stand there so long my mom knocks on the door to ask if I'm okay, and I tell her I am fine.

Afterward, I go to my bed and fall asleep, wrapped in a towel. When my mother wakes me, it is already dark, and Jed is waiting downstairs.

It is only later, many years later, that I will think about why we didn't go to the cemetery. When I think about this, I think about my mother, whose own mother died when she was thirteen, whose mother had been sick since my mother could remember. Maybe my mother didn't want to think about another daughter becoming motherless. Maybe she didn't want to see another mother's body being lowered into the ground.

Jed takes me to see a Disney movie to cheer me up. There are singing candlesticks and talking teacups and a beast who's really a beauty underneath. After the movie, we drive around for a while, looking for a spot, our old habit. He tells me about school, and then he pulls up at the edge of an out-of-the-way street and puts the car into park.

He puts his hands around my waist. I know he isn't my boyfriend anymore, but that doesn't matter because now he is kissing me, now he is running his hands up and down my legs, now he is putting his hands in my hair. Finally, I can breathe, finally I can close my eyes, finally I can disappear completely.

There's still one more night, one more night when it's winter, even though it's already been winter for so long. One night in winter when I am seventeen, and it's the middle of the night, and it's snowing outside, which I know immediately, even though I am barely awake.

I hear noises coming from the kitchen—that's what wakes me—and I walk downstairs.

My mother is in a corner of the kitchen. She is huddled in a corner, cowering. She looks afraid, more afraid than I've ever seen her look, and I have seen her look afraid many times.

My father is in the kitchen also. It is because he's in the kitchen that my mother is afraid. It is because he is throwing chairs at her. There are kitchen chairs, and they're being thrown at my mother, who has cowered her way into a corner. What choice does she have if there are chairs involved? My mother does not look beautiful in this scene. She has lost her beauty; she has given it up in exchange for something else. Her face is gray, her hair is gray. She is wearing what she wears to sleep, a sweatshirt and a slip.

She is screaming. Now she is a screamer like me.

My father is screaming too. And what he's screaming is, "You frigid, sexless bitch. You cold, frigid bitch."

"You don't know how to be a wife," he screams at her. "If you don't want me to be your husband, I won't be. If this is what you want instead, this is what you will get."

I have heard these words so many times. They are not words I want to hear, they are not words a daughter should ever have to hear. A young daughter does not know what these words mean, but I am no longer a young daughter, and I know what they mean.

There are screams coming out of the house, but for once, they're not mine. I am standing and watching. I have a younger sister and three little brothers, but none of them wakes, nobody stirs. Aside from the screaming and the sound of the kitchen chairs as they hit the tile, the house is silent.

There is something that clicks over in me now. I see my mother in the kitchen, and things lock into place. Something opens up.

I go back to my room and find the car keys in the dark in the pocket of my winter coat. I don't have time to put on the coat or a pair of shoes, even though it's snowing. I need to move silently, as silently as I can.

I creep down the stairs. I open the front door. I do not make a noise. Outside it is snowing, and I am wearing just a T-shirt and underwear. My feet are bare. I will feel the accelerator under my bare foot; I will feel what I am doing.

I turn on the engine. I am not cold. The car knows what to do; it moves fast and quiet like me. I pull out of the driveway, and I drive. I know where I am going, and I keep driving until I get there.

I drive the car fast. I do not stop for lights. The streets are empty. My mind is empty. It is cold and clear and brilliant in its emptiness. I drive, and I keep driving until I get where I am going.

It is still the middle of the night; it is still the same night, but it is so much night that it's now closer to morning. There have been police cars, more than one, parked on our street since I drove to the police station and told them to follow me home. The police have stood in our living room, while my father hides upstairs. The police have been at our house, but there has not been an arrest. The police can only take action based on what they see with their own eyes. Unless my mother wants to press charges, but she cannot do that; of course, she cannot do that.

These men speak in short words. They ask simple questions. One of them asks, "Has this happened before?" and my mother says, "Yes, it's been happening for years." The policeman asks, "Are you going to leave him?" and my mother looks straight ahead. I can see something uncloud in her too, something turn hard, and she says, "Yes. Yes, I am leaving him."

She does not speak in the future tense or the past tense. She speaks in the present tense, as though it is something that's already happening, something that has already been set into motion, something that once set off, cannot be reversed.

After a while, my mother tells the police they can leave, and after a while, they do.

They give her a card, a card with a number to call. They say to call anytime.

When it is almost light out, and still very cold, the police leave our house. My father is still up in his room, but my mother and I are not afraid. We have the beginnings of a plan, where we will go from here. Something has been broken tonight, something has cracked open.

Soon my father wakes up, not that he was sleeping. He comes downstairs to the living room, where my mother and I are talking. By now, I have put on some clothes. My father does not speak to my mother because he can see this is not her doing. My father speaks to me. He has some things he'd like to say.

"You think you're very smart, don't you?" my father says. "You think you are smarter than anyone else. You think it's a clever trick to go get the police, to call the police on your own father. You think that's a good trick."

He is looking straight at me because why should he be afraid? I am a seventeen-year-old girl in the middle of the night.

"Let me tell you something," my father says. "The police will not protect you. They don't care about you."

My father is looking straight at me. Why should he be afraid?

"If you want to play a game, I can play a game too. If you think it's fun to hurt your own father, if you think that is smart, I can be smart too."

Now my father produces something from his pocket, the pocket of his bathrobe.

It's a piece of paper. The paper is folded. My father unfolds the piece of paper. My mother does not move.

My father turns toward my mother. He says, "You are a cold fish, but your daughter is very friendly."

My father holds the paper, creased with unfolded lines, and begins to read. "Dear . . ." he reads, and he fills in the name of the boy I went to middle school with, the boy who read me the story over the phone, the boy who asked me to write him this letter, this letter I never gave him because after I had hidden it in the back of my closet, behind my winter sweaters, I could not find it again. And because I could not find it, I believed I had imagined it. I told myself I had made it up.

Now I know I did not make it up because I can see the letter in my father's hands.

My father reads on. He reads aloud. The things I wrote I wanted to do to the boy who had told me what I wanted to do to him. I am a writer, and now my father can see the proof. I am smart, but I am not quick. If I were quick, I never would have let my father read in the first place. But it's hard to stop a story once it's started, to interrupt a reader who's begun to read.

All the snow from outside has come into our living room and melted. There's a flood in the house, which explains why I am underwater. My father, my mother, and I are drowning because I cannot move fast enough.

My father turns to my mother. He says, "You could learn a thing or two from your daughter. She is very friendly. She is a whore."

Soon I come to and grab the letter from my father. He has only managed to read the first few lines. I shred the letter with my hands and leave the pieces burning in my palm. My mother has gone blank. She is staring straight ahead.

Once the snow stopped falling, the stars had come out. I could see that. Even from inside the living room, I could see that.

It was a holy night. My mother and father were there that night, my three sleeping brothers, my sleeping sister, my ancestors, all the men who would ever try to love me and all the men I would ever try to love. Also God. God always comes to see the transformation from innocence into something else.

I have to get out of the house. And so I walk outside while it is still so late it is not yet morning, and I stand beneath a streetlamp, and I pray.

Please God, please God, please. Please God, help me, please God, help me, please just help me God, please.

Even now, I can still see the single spaceship glow of the suburban streetlight, the only thing illuminating the darkness of the street. I can still remember when I closed my eyes and whispered, "God, if you help me survive this, I promise I will devote my life to you."

7

A WOMAN OF VALOR, WHO CAN FIND?

AFTER MY MOM FILES THE PAPERS, things get worse. For one thing, my father starts to tell my mother he will kill her. Not that the idea is new. What is new is the clarity with which he expresses the idea.

"The next time you leave this house will be in a body bag," he says.

The fact that my father wants to kill my mother is something I have always known, but now he is saying it out loud. "The next time you leave this house will be in a body bag." The more he says it, the more I believe it.

It gets bad enough that my mom takes us to her brother's house, to Uncle Peter and Auntie Lily's, two towns over. It is a house with a marble foyer, a house with leather chairs, a house where you press a button and music pipes into the pool area. How many Mother's Days, Father's Days, birthdays did I spend at this house, sitting on the yellow lounge chair with my library book, while I was supposed to be in the pool having fun?

My mother grew up in this house, at least for the part of her life after her mother died. A big marble-floored house, where she was left alone until her brother bought it from my grandfather. On those endless Sunday afternoons, I'd watch while my dad tried to make conversation with Uncle Peter by sharing bits of the research he'd done on the history of their family name, tracing its origins from medieval Germany.

My father has made his livelihood on the premise that he is connected to the past, to a long stretch of history going backward through time, but my uncle has no interest in the past; he has succeeded in this world and cannot be impressed. For years, I've watched my father endure these Sunday afternoons at Uncle Peter and Aunt Lily's, knowing he was the only one who felt as out of place as I did.

Uncle Peter and Auntie Lily have a daughter a few years older than me—my cousin, Sloan, who is already away at college, where she's pledged Sigma Delta Tau. It is her room that I stay in, her room that will be mine until we can go home.

Sloan's shelves are lined with gymnastics trophies and group photos where the girls all wear leotards. Above the bed is a nearly life-size portrait of her, commissioned on the occasion of her bat mitzvah. The dusty-rose walls match the dusty-rose carpet, all off-set by low modern furniture.

In the marble-floored hallway, there are dozens of photographs, a whole wall of photographs. Pictures of Uncle Peter and Auntie Lily and Sloan and her brother, Henry—skiing in Aspen, at a beach in Maui, at a country-club dinner. The only pictures are pictures of themselves. You can easily see in the pictures that Sloan's skin has always been the same shade of golden honey, no matter what the season. It's not just because they have more money that they seem happier, I think. It's because they actually are.

After a few days, we return home. My father promises he won't be crazy, but every night, I hear my parents arguing. My father does not want a divorce; why would he? He is the rabbi, my mother is the rabbi's wife, and we are the rabbi's children. Nobody at the synagogue knows what happens in our home, and it had to stay that way. A rabbi getting divorced isn't like a shoe salesman getting divorced, my mother always told me. It throws everything into question. It undermines every claim.

"I'll lose my job," my father yells. "Is that what you want? To take that away from me too?"

Other nights, I hear him speaking calmly, trying to build his case. What they need to do is work on their marriage, he tells my mother, just the two of them. No lawyers, no therapists, no police officers. That's the problem, he tells her. She's always trying to involve other people.

That's what's so upsetting to him, he tells her; that's why he's so angry. If she would stop running off to her brother's house, if she would stop telling the whole world their problems, everything would be fine.

My mom doesn't have a mom, so she calls my father's mom, who of course wants to help.

At night, as I'm falling asleep, I can hear my mom crying on the phone to my grandmother in New York City, who loves my mother like her very own daughter. Other nights, she calls her father, who lives in the California desert, surrounded by lemon and kumquat trees.

What we need is a plan, and that's what my mom and I are making, in the kitchen table at night after the kids have gone to sleep. Obviously, we will have to move; how could we stay in the house six blocks from my father's synagogue? How could we pass former congregants in the produce section at the supermarket? My mother will no longer be the rabbi's wife, and I will no longer be the rabbi's daughter. We will both be something else.

We will have to move, but where? My grandfather will help financially, but it will not be simple. My mother will be answerable to her father, she tells me. She will have to account for every one of her choices.

"I'll exchange one cage for another," she tells me one night. "At least with your father, he doesn't care what I do."

We could move to a small apartment on the west side of the city, I tell my mom. It won't be easy, but together we can do it. I will get a job, I tell her, I will help with expenses. I can enroll at the local community college, I tell my mom. I can live at home to save money. I can help with the kids.

As for my father, he has made it clear that if my mother follows through with the divorce, he will not grant it. He will refuse her petition, which, according to Jewish law, is his right. He will make my mother an *aguna*, a woman relegated to purgatorial status, neither married nor divorced, chained to a husband who does not want her, but will not set her free.

My father says he will move to Jerusalem and never come back.

"What about your children?" my mother says.

"You have poisoned my children against me," he says.

And suddenly I understand. That Jerusalem is not just a city, but a refuge of the imagination, a place to disappear to.

There was a new teacher at school that year. Mrs. Zimmermann had come from Bais Yaakov, the ultra-Orthodox girls' school whose rules made those at the Academy look lenient. There was a rumor she'd had a falling-out with the administration, which was surprising since she'd been there for years, teaching through all her ten pregnancies.

Mrs. Zimmermann was the daughter of a great rabbi, the descendant of a whole line of rabbis, heads of the yeshivas in Poland before everything was destroyed. She was also the wife of one of the city's most respected rabbis, a revered scholar whose name invoked solemnity. There was another rumor about Mrs. Zimmermann: that she herself was a Torah scholar, with a body of knowledge no less encyclopedic than her husband's, that after she put all ten of her children to bed, she stayed up studying Torah, subsisting on only a few hours of sleep.

She is my teacher for Prophets, and this semester we are studying the Book of Proverbs, written by King Solomon. She stands before us, the Book of Proverbs open in her hand, and begins to read, but she cannot read because she cannot contain her excitement, her astonishment at the poetry.

"Girls, listen to this," she says. "This is so *gevaldig*, you have to listen close."

She's the only teacher I've ever had who talks like this, who speaks about texts with love.

The way her voice rises when she starts to read faster, her heavy Ashkenazi pronunciation flattening all the vowels, makes every word seem like a glowing jewel.

We've arrived at chapter 31. Everyone knows how it starts: *A woman of valor, who can find? Her price is far above rubies.* But then it goes on:

Her husband's heart trusts her / he will lack no fortune.

She repays his good but never his bad all the days of her life.

She seeks out wool and linen / her hands work eagerly.

This passage is the same passage that's recited every Friday night, sung after the song welcoming the Sabbath angels, but before the blessing over the wine. Throughout the centuries, Jewish husbands have sung this song to their wives on Friday nights, after the candles have been lit, but before the bread is blessed. Except in our home. I have never once heard these words pass my father's lips.

But here is Mrs. Zimmermann—a rabbi's wife, a mother of ten children, a scholar of Torah. In her strawberry-blond wig and pleated skirt, she could almost pass for a student. She stays up late at night preparing for our class, she tells us, because she loves the words so much. She says she will give extra credit to anyone who memorizes all twenty-two verses.

I want to raise my hand, because I want to ask a question. The question I want to ask is about expectations. The woman of valor arises while it is still nighttime, she plants a vineyard, she extends her palm to the poor. Her children praise her. Her husband extols her virtues.

I want to ask Mrs. Zimmermann if she thinks it's reasonable—that a woman should be responsible for maintaining the household, bringing in an income, raising the children, that only through diligence can she earn her husband's respect. I keep my hand up, but Mrs. Zimmermann doesn't notice, and after a while, I put it down. I know she will not understand my question—the questioning of a role I should be grateful for.

I count the days until Auntie Sonia arrives. She is coming to move my father out, to find him a place of his own. It sounds impossible, like a dream or a fairy tale: my mother and father's house without my father in it. I don't know how Auntie Sonia will do it, only that she's the only person who can do it. My father's older sister by two years, she is the only person in the world he respects.

Once Auntie Sonia is here, I tell myself, everything will be made real. She will make my father understand the facts in front of him; she will make him see he has no choice. She will pack up his suits and his books. She will fix his delusions, the same as she fixed the peeling wallpaper in our kitchen four summers ago: by stripping the walls clean and painting them a calming, neutral shade.

One Tuesday in the late winter, just before spring, I come home from school and Auntie Sonia is there. My father's still at work, but she is drinking coffee with my mother in the living room. She is wearing something vintage, like always, in this case a man's beige cardigan with red and navy trim, tucked into high-waisted slacks.

"I love your sweater," I say.

"You can have it, dolly," she says. "I'll bring it for you the next time I see you. I think it's from the forties, but the man at the shop kept trying to convince me it was the fifties. What does he know?"

I know that Auntie Sonia doesn't have much time to spend with me on this trip, because she will be busy talking to my parents.

One night, I hear the three of them in the kitchen. I tiptoe out of bed and lean over the metal banister, the star of the suburban split-level. I can see Auntie Sonia at the head of the table, my mother and father sitting across from her like schoolchildren. It is late at night; no one expects me to be up. More likely, no one is thinking about me at all. I can hear some of the words, but not others, I can see Auntie Sonia explaining something, but I can't hear what.

The next day, Auntie Sonia says she'd like some time alone with me. "Just the two of us," she says, and asks if I'd like to join her for tea in the lobby of the Marriott where she's staying.

When I arrive, she is already there, a white teapot on the table in front of her, two Lipton tea bags on a saucer. She gets to the point.

"I don't know if you've heard, dolly, but your parents have decided to stay together."

I am wearing the sweater she gave me. I hear the words she's saying, but not their meanings.

"What are you talking about?" I say, and she tells me about how there are still very young children at home, how things are more complicated than they seem, how my mom and dad have talked things out.

Now I understand the meaning of the words that she is saying, or at least their partial meanings, but mostly I feel cold. Even as I hold a hot cup of tea, the warmth drains out of me. My hands go numb, and my vision blurs.

I think of the letter I received in the mail from my grandmother just a few weeks earlier, the one that began *Sara darling*, as every letter I've ever received from her does.

> Your time at home is limited now to mere months, and my sense of a household besieged by past injustices, retaliations, and defense mechanisms fills me with as deep a sadness as I have ever known. My darling, only your Mom and Dad themselves can break the vicious cycle that is closing in around this family. It is between THEM alone, and not the role of the children to judge and put blame all on one parent—and therefore side with and love only the other

parent. I know it is difficult for a young person to understand what isolation is—and how much your father needs
your support and respect. A situation such as this is always
easier for the woman, and it is my prayer, now as you stand
on the brink of your beautiful young womanhood, to recognize the pain your Dad is going thru, and to be there for him
as well as your Mom. I love you always.

Your Nana

I think about the report I've been working on for my mom's
lawyer, the one that charts the dates and times of my father's violence. I made the list in blue pen, based on accounts from my
diary going back to fifth grade. Lately, my mom has been talking
about getting a restraining order, but first she needs proof.

"That's impossible," I say to Auntie Sonia, and I don't care if
my voice is raised. "My mom and I have already talked about it.
We already have a plan."

"Your parents still want to be married," she says. "I know it's
been difficult, and your father's been under a lot of stress at the
temple, but he's going to be better. He's made that commitment."

"But *how* will he be better?" I ask. "Will he see a psychologist?
Will he get some kind of help?"

And it is here that I can see her face change, her face that
looks so much like mine. Up until now, she has been generous to
me, but I have reached the limits of her generosity. She doesn't
like the specificity of my questions, my negative attitude.

"You're only seventeen," she says. "There are things that go
on between a husband and wife that you cannot understand."

And, in that moment, I realize that it's already been undone.
All my talks with my mom, the list I made for the lawyer with

the dates and descriptions of events. How I could almost see the apartment we would rent, the kids cozy in their rooms, my mom making dinner while I set the table, both of us knowing we did the hardest thing together.

Even now, it makes me angry. Even now, I wish I could go back and find the girl I used to be and tell her that everything she thinks is wrong is wrong, that everything she thinks she knows, she knows.

When I think back now on the night at the Marriott, I can't remember if I said goodbye to Auntie Sonia, if I hugged or kissed her, how I drove home. I cannot remember anything else that happened that night, because all I can remember is the feeling of being trapped underwater, where it doesn't matter what you say or how loudly you say it, because nobody can hear you.

After Auntie Sonia leaves, I stop going to school. There's no point, and I can't stand it anymore. The endless drive on the expressway, all the cars. The long days in the concrete building listening to teachers talk about nothing so they can feel important. I don't want to go to school anymore, and so I stop going.

After Auntie Sonia leaves, I get into a fight with my mom.

"How can you do this?" I say. "I don't understand."

"It's a three-month reconciliation period," she says. "Your father's agreed to make changes. Things will be different," she says. "Your father will be better."

What she means is she's afraid. What she means is she is traumatized. What she means is she has no self-esteem. I will come to understand this when I'm older. Even now I understand this in some way, but it does not touch my fury.

"How can you do this?" I scream, and then I go upstairs and cry on my bed, because there's nowhere else to go.

My anger could fill an ocean, a continent, a book. It could topple a mountain or burn down a building. Instead, it fills my body.

At night, I look in the mirror. My skin is getting worse. I've stopped taking the antibiotics the doctor prescribed because they turned my face leathery and gave me stomachaches. Now my skin is filled with pustules, some like mountains, some like craters. The toxins are filling up my body, and there's nowhere for them to go.

In our house, things continue as they always have. My father leaving for prayer services in the morning, visiting the hospitalized in the afternoons, my mother doing the grocery shopping and folding the laundry. As though nothing ever happened, as though everything is fine.

I am staying up later and later. Since I've stopped going to school, it doesn't matter, and I've come to like the quiet. Late at night, I lock the bathroom door and stare into the mirror. I survey the damage from the previous night—the half-drained pimple on my left cheek, now infected; the scab at the crease of my chin I'm already peeling off; all the tiny divots where I've tried to extract the poison.

When I finish, I see what I've done, the changing topography of my face. Some of the wounds have started to heal, but the new ones are still bleeding.

In the middle of the night, I sit up in my bed and scream. I cannot help it. I think I am asleep, and maybe I am—but suddenly I'm awake, sitting ramrod straight, and screaming. My sister is in the bed across from mine—of course she is, since it's her room too—and when I scream, I wake her.

"Shut up!" she screams. "What's wrong with you!"

But I am seventeen, and she is fourteen, and she has no idea.

"Stop screaming!" she screams, but I cannot stop.

"You're crazy!" she says, and I know that she is right. There is no question she is right, and I make no effort to correct her.

I haven't been to school in weeks—the days bleed into each other, while I watch reruns of my favorite drama on the Lifetime channel. My parents don't seem to notice that I'm not in school, or else they do not care. They have more pressing concerns, like trying to keep their lives from crumbling around them.

My friends don't seem to notice either. There is a heaviness about me that didn't used to be there, a veil of darkness they cannot name, but they can feel. Good religious girls from good religious families, like Shayna and Batsheva, don't want to be reminded of any bad things in the world; they are too busy leading a life designed to keep them wholesome and protected.

When you're a seventeen-year-old religious girl and bad things happen to you, your friends don't tell you why they've stopped talking to you; they just disappear.

During the mornings, the house is quiet, but in the afternoons, the phone starts ringing. We don't have caller ID, so there's no way to know who it is. One afternoon, I let the phone ring, but my mother calls out to me to pick it up. So I do, and right away, I know it's a mistake.

"*Sara?*" the voice says, the *r* guttural, the vowels clipped. She is saying my name in Hebrew, which sounds like a different name entirely.

"Yes?" I say. And I immediately regret identifying myself.

"*Lamah at lo b'beit sefer?*" the voice demands.

She wants to know why I am not at school. So I tell her the same thing I do when I call the school office in the mornings: that I'm not feeling well, that I have not been feeling well for a long time. I hope she will respond with sympathy, but this is Giveret Orenberg, and she knows that I am lying.

It's hard to remember now, but months ago, I'd asked her to write me a college recommendation letter. I had done exceptionally well in her class, diagramming entire Hebrew sentences according to their grammatical structure, with variations for gender and tense. When I'd asked her to write it, she'd willingly agreed.

But it is this very letter she now wants to take back. She reminds me that I have not turned in my paper on Bialik, which was due the previous week, that I missed the midterm grammar test. She says she will write to the colleges I've applied to and revoke her recommendation.

I tell her I am working on the Bialik paper, another lie, and that I can come in to make up the midterm on Monday, to which she begrudgingly agrees.

When I hang up the phone, I am shaking. I don't want to go back to school, but I have to go back to school. It's just for a day, I tell myself, then I'll never go back again. But I can't go to school with my face looking like this, with my insides erupting on the surface. I can't go to school looking like this, like I've been afflicted with leprosy. There is only one solution: I will have to cover it up.

And so I drive to the drugstore, where I buy a trifecta of products that promise to *Hide it while you heal it!* as though this has anything to do with healing. I don't want to be alive, but the next best thing is to be invisible, and so, the next morning, in the dark of my room before I leave for school, I apply the makeup in layers:

first the concealer, then the foundation, then the matte powder. I look in the mirror, satisfied. Nobody can see my pimples. They can barely see me at all.

My first-period class is Prophets with Mrs. Zimmermann. Today, she is returning to the beginning of the Book of Proverbs to review before the midterm. She holds her book aloft as she reads aloud: "Listen, my son, to your father's instruction and do not forsake your mother's teaching. They are a garland to grace your head and a chain to adorn your neck . . ."

After class, as I'm walking out, Mrs. Zimmermann touches me on the arm and asks me to stay back. When the other students have filed out, she looks at me with her hazel eyes.

"Sarahleh," she says, "you haven't been in class for a while. How are you?"

There is something about the way she is looking at me that makes me want to tell her the truth. But as soon as I open my mouth, my eyes fill up, and I cannot speak.

"Come see me during lunch," she says. "Then we can talk."

When 12:30 comes, I sit with Mrs. Zimmermann on the wooden bench outside her classroom. She opens a small bag of potato chips, which she explains is her lunch.

I tell her about the police. About my father telling me to drop dead. About waking up in the middle of the night screaming. I tell her everything. Everything except the part about the letter and the name my father called me.

"Where is your father now?" she asks.

"He's still in the house."

"Saraleh," she says, "you should come stay by me. You and your mother and your brothers and sister."

I think of what I know about her: that she has ten children, that she stays up all night reading the books of the Prophets.

"I don't think you would have room for us," I say.

She waves her hand. "*Shtus*," she says. "We will make room."

I think about her offer. How my family has failed, failed to bring light into the world, but also failed at the most basic thing: to be happy. And now we belong nowhere. I think about my mother, the rabbi's wife, living under the roof of another rabbi's wife.

"I don't think that would work," I tell Mrs. Zimmermann.

"You don't have to tell me in advance," she says. "Just come." She writes down her address on a piece of paper and gives it to me.

"At least come for Shabbos," she says. "You'll come stay by me this Shabbos."

At Mrs. Zimmermann's house, her daughters buzz around her like bees. One chopping onions for the egg salad, another feeding the baby with a bottle, another setting the table with crystal wineglasses.

When shul is over, Rabbi Zimmermann walks through the door in his *kapota*, his full-length black silk jacket, and his tall black Borsolino.

The first person he looks at is Mrs. Zimmermann.

"Good Shabbos, Good Shabbos," he says, his daughters swarming around him, darting in and out of the kitchen, bringing out dish after dish.

During the meal, Rabbi Zimmermann gives a *dvar Torah*, an overview of what the commentators have to say about this week's Torah portion. Then he sings a wordless *nigun*, or melody, as his

children gaze at him with love. This is the first time I have seen
another rabbi's family up close. Watching Rabbi Zimmermann at
the head of his Shabbos table, I realize that, compared to Rabbi
Zimmermann, my father is not a rabbi at all. He is barely a man.

And I realize in that moment too, that my parents have sold
me a mirage, a facsimile of the real thing, which I am seeing now
for the first time. A wife steeped in language, in the holiness of
the book; a husband who, by virtue of his wisdom and purity of
heart, has earned the respect not just of his congregation, but,
more crucially, of his family; an eldest daughter who does not
hate herself because she is not keeping anyone's secrets. This was
a real rabbi's family, the kind my parents wished we could be.

A religious life, I saw now, demands a singularity of purpose
that my parents did not possess. Mrs. Zimmermann's daughters
do not know who Madonna is because they don't own a television.
Nor were they permitted to mix with boys. No, Mrs. Zimmermann was in the business of protecting her daughters, which is
why, when they turned eighteen or nineteen, they would begin
going on arranged dates with the purpose of getting married and
building a home of faith.

This is what I want. Now that I have seen the real article, I
can no longer be fooled.

Two weeks later, I receive a letter of acceptance from the college
that is my top choice, the one I have been working the past four
years to get into. But I will not be attending college in the fall,
because I have decided instead to go to Jerusalem. I've enrolled
myself at a women's seminary, one of the most respected in the
city, where I will immerse myself in Torah, the books of Prophets
and Writings, the encyclopedic tractates of Jewish law. I will live

in a dormitory with other young women, not far from where I was born.

I imagine walking to the apartment where my parents used to live, the one I've only seen in pictures, bougainvillea spilling over the third-floor balcony where my mother holds me in a swaddle. I understand now that my parents did not make a mistake when they decided to devote their lives to God; their mistake was not devoting themselves fully. They'd stopped somewhere in the middle, because in their hearts they were selfish—too selfish to make themselves into vessels for God's will.

But I will be different. I will leave this place, with its faux Tudor mansions encircled by malls, and I will go to the place God has shown me. I will go to Jerusalem to study God's words, just like I promised that night beneath the streetlight. The Five Books of Moses, the many books of Prophets, the commentaries upon commentaries upon commentaries. I will stay late in the study hall, reading and praying. I will purify myself with God's words and emerge someone new.

PART II

You Shall Have
No Other Gods Before Me

8

ALL THE GLORY OF THE KING'S DAUGHTER IS WITHIN

I WAS THE MOST BEAUTIFUL BRIDE in the world. You don't have to take my word for it. Look at the pictures. There I am, my dark hair pulled back into a simple ponytail, my skin finally clear, pearls hand-embroidered along the edge of my veil, a sheaf of cream and lavender lisianthus cradled in my arms like a baby. As a bride, I didn't become someone else, I just looked the way I always imagined I would have looked if nothing bad had ever happened to me. My green eyes matched the trees that were the backdrop for the wedding portraits, my lips barely open, as though to pose a question.

In accordance with Jewish law, I had spent the day fasting, reciting the Yom Kippur service from a white leather prayer book inscribed with gold lettering. One's wedding day is likened to the Day of Judgment, a day when you pray for forgiveness, when all your sins are wiped clean.

Both my parents were there the day of my wedding, alive and still married, with sparkling white teeth, my father in an expensive dark suit, my mother in a seafoam silk dress and matching jacket she'd had custom made for the occasion. They escorted me to the wedding canopy, my father on my right side, my mother on my left, a candle protected by hurricane glass in each of their hands. The sun began to set, and a breeze blew in from the Judaean Hills. The words from the Book of Jeremiah rose up all around us. *The sounds of joy and gladness, the voices of bride and bridegroom.*

I was twenty-six the day that I got married. Most of my friends had been married for years, some already had babies. Even my little sister had gotten married before me. I entertained the idea that God had forgotten me. Or that I was undeserving of love, which amounted to the same thing. For years, I'd been living in Jerusalem, waiting to be chosen. You might think that I'd be cynical about marriage, but that was not the case. Marriage was what I dreamed of, what I prayed for. I knew my parents had done it wrong. I wanted to purify it, make it holy.

The previous night, I had gone to the ritual bath for the first time, accompanied by my mother and sister. I already knew what to do from the bridal classes I'd been taking for the last six weeks. The plucking and shaving and filing and combing and sloughing required prior to immersion. The inspection of the bride's body for a speck of dirt, a stray hair, a ragged fingernail—anything that had the power to render the immersion invalid.

Nothing could come between a bride and the holy waters of the ritual bath. The water had to touch you everywhere.

As I stood naked at the edge, before I descended, the bath attendant entered the room to inspect me.

"What a beautiful bride," she said.

My mother started to cry.

My sister cried too.

Then I went under, remembering to keep my hands unclenched, my limbs extended, my palms open, so that the water could touch every part of me. These waters, my bridal instructor had taught me, were the secret to a life of blessing, healthy children, a peaceful home. They would make every time like the first time. They would make me beloved.

The band played all night, and all night I danced under the stars in the hills ringing Jerusalem. I danced with my mother, my mother-in-law, my sister-in-law, and my sister, seven months pregnant in a multicolored stone necklace I'd helped her groom pick out the previous summer. My new husband, he danced too, on the other side with my father and his father and my brothers and all the men. And when the band burst into streams of mandolin and banjo, I suddenly found myself past the *mechitza* dividing the men from the women, and my new husband's face caught mine, and without my knowing or thinking, we were dancing together, a chain of men forming concentric circles around us in the cooled heat of the June night, and I thought, I have never been so happy in my life.

It was not on our wedding night that Adam and I first came to know each other as husband and wife. That happened the following morning in the shower of the King David Hotel, the hot water rushing over my head as my husband touched all the places that, until the previous night, had been forbidden.

"You're perfect," he said, and in that moment, I believed him.

Afterward, we had breakfast in our room, paper-thin omelets flecked with herbs, fresh melon and sliced oranges and pomegranate seeds, pastries served with fig jam and date honey.

On our first date, Adam and I had gone to the Western Wall. It was the first night of Selichot, the days of repentance leading up to Rosh Hashanah, and he wanted to know if I wanted to go to the Western Wall with him, and, without hesitation, I said yes, because ever since we had met at the going-away party of a mutual friend, I'd been waiting for him to call.

By the time I met Adam, I'd been living in Jerusalem for three years, having first come to the city to study in a women's seminary when I was seventeen. I'd gone back to America only to attend college, which I completed as quickly as I could, counting the days until I could return to Jerusalem's stone streets and pine forests.

On the night of our first date, the Western Wall Plaza was filled with Jews who'd come to pray. Old women with their heads covered, mothers pushing strollers, little boys with sidelocks holding their fathers' hands—all of them illuminated by the overhead stadium lights against the night. Adam and I descended the stone steps, worn slippery from use but not as slippery as they'd be during the rainy season. We descended another set of steps, and another, and another, our steps falling into sync with each other until we reached the place where we would have to separate, men to the left side, women to the right.

"Pray as long as you need to," Adam said, which made me want to marry him.

Through trial and error, I had learned that I could only a trust a man who had accepted the yoke of heaven, a man who wanted to be as close to God as I did.

After we prayed, Adam and I walked through the Old City's alleyways, nearly empty at this hour. He told me about growing up in Vermont, about the quietness of snowshoeing through freshly fallen snow. He told me about not knowing he was Jewish, not really, about not even knowing what that meant. The snow was his religion. The mountains, too. He told me about traveling anywhere, everywhere, but nothing had held him as Jerusalem had. Something in the air was different here; he knew that right away. When a stranger at the Western Wall invited him for Shabbat dinner, something in him changed forever.

All this was still new to him, all this that was so known to me.

Adam did not like to discuss the past—his last girlfriend, why his parents got divorced, the reason he was raised by a single father. It wasn't that he spoke badly of his family so much as he spoke of them with no particular feeling at all. "I'm with you now," he would say if I tried to press further. "You are all that matters."

What I knew was that he wanted our family to be different. A home filled with children and the Sabbath and Torah study and God. He knew I was the person he wanted to build that home with because that was the thing I wanted too.

Now it was the day after our wedding, and it was already past checkout time. On account of the recent bombings, the hotel was nearly empty, and they'd allowed us to extend our stay. But we couldn't extend our stay indefinitely. Soon we'd have to leave the hotel and begin our married life.

And so I wrapped my hair in a plum-colored scarf, twisting its long ends to frame my face, just as I'd been practicing in the mirror for months. I put on a cotton shirt and a dark purple skirt with purple flowers, and my husband took a photograph of me sitting on the rumpled bedsheets. We went to the front desk to return the key. Then we stepped out of the hotel and into the blinding Jerusalem sun.

It is Friday afternoon, and everyone is coming to our apartment for Shabbat dinner. My sister and her husband and baby, who live on the other side of the city in the run-down neighborhood outside the souk, and my two brothers, Joseph and Ephraim, who were studying at a well-known yeshiva in the Old City. Only our baby brother, Noam, was still at home with our parents, on the other side of the world.

One by one, my parents' children—first me, then Rachel, then Joseph, then Ephraim—had moved to Jerusalem, the city we had prayed to every day of our lives, the city we'd invoked every time we said the Grace After Meals and the Eighteen Blessings, the city we'd been raised to believe could save us. And it was in this city, far from home, that we had taken on more commandments, finding refuge and rebellion in our devotion to God. My brothers had stopped wearing khakis and now only wore dark pants with white button-downs, and large velvet kippahs. My sister and I had given up jeans and tank tops, and now wore only long skirts and dresses.

Were we running away from something, or did we love God that much? Like you could even separate the two.

To prepare for the Sabbath, I had cleaned the apartment, baked a fish, roasted several eggplants, and prepared a tableful of salads. Adam was a vegetarian, and I tried to make him happy. I'd plugged in the hot-water urn and the electric hot plate so the food could be kept warm. I'd put the lights on timers, unscrewed the light bulb in the refrigerator, and hidden the computer away in a cupboard. I did all the things I'd watched my mother do, and more.

The summer had already passed, and so had the High Holy Days. The air in Jerusalem was getting colder, especially at night. It had gotten cold enough that I'd asked Adam to turn on the heater, a 1950s model that ran on kerosene and leaked acrid fumes. In the whole city, there was only one repairman who still serviced the old kerosene models, but he was fully booked until the following week.

"The smell is giving me a headache," I tell Adam.

"I'll open the windows," he says.

Because our guests are my family, I do not have to cover my hair—at least not within the four walls of my home. This alone puts me in a good mood. The Torah teaches that a married woman's head covering is a crown that brings honor to herself, to her husband, to the entire Jewish people. In the first few months of marriage, I had loved wrapping my head in a scarf. But with summer, that feeling had faded, and what came in its place was the inability to recognize the woman I saw in the mirror.

Before meeting Adam, I'd always allowed myself the requisite loopholes. There were a handful of occasions on which I'd eaten food that was not certified kosher, times when I'd broken the Sabbath. In moments of great weakness, I had transgressed the injunction not to touch members of the opposite sex. But Adam did not believe in loopholes; he believed in following the letter of the law.

Through the kitchen window, I can see the sun creeping low, threatening to set. My sister arrives with her husband and baby and pack-n-play and knapsack full of cloth diapers, just in time for candlelighting, which in Jerusalem comes earlier than anywhere else. My brothers, freshly showered and dressed in the black pants and white button-down of the yeshiva student, arrive soon after, Joseph bearing a box of cookies.

"Wow, it smells so good in here," he says.

"Did you make the eggplant dip?" Ephraim says. "That's my favorite."

When my brothers are around is when I feel most useful. I could cook for them and do their laundry and let them bring their friends over for *Shalosh seudos*, the Sabbath's final meal. I could do all the things I'd always wanted to do for them but had never been able to—to show them a home where things are okay, where no one is afraid. We are still within the window before *shkia*, the time when the ball of the sun falls below the horizon, which means Joseph still has time to go into the kitchen and make himself one last cup of coffee.

My sister and I light the candles, bringing our hands over our eyes in three swift motions, and recite the blessing. Then our brothers and husbands leave for synagogue, the one just up the hill from our apartment.

With the men gone, my sister arranges a blanket over her shoulder and brings her baby to her breast. Unlike my sister, I'd never fantasized about motherhood, never felt its visceral pull. Adam and I had asked a local rabbinic figure for a six-month dispensation to use birth control. The dispensation was running out, and I wanted to ask for another.

My sister fishes two *People* magazines out of her diaper bag, contraband borrowed from her friend Zeisi, and the chewy German candies for which she'd always had a weakness.

"Give me the gossip," I say to her. "Give me all of it."

All our lives, my sister and I had shared a room; all the closeness had made us distant. It was only on the other side of the world that we had come to know each other, that we had space to breathe.

By the time the men return, it is already dark. Adam recites the kiddush over the wine, the *hamotzi* blessing over the bread, the guttural sounds of the holy language still new to him. I'd cooked all the food, but it was Adam who baked the bread, experimenting with different ratios of rye and spelt. He'd dusted his loaves with sunflower and poppy seeds, their dense, nutty flesh yielding to the knife after he blessed them. While we eat, my sister tells a story about breaking down on the highway years ago in the middle of a snowstorm on her way to Wisconsin.

". . . but then it turned out it was a state trooper!" she says, and we all laugh, especially Joseph, who always laughs the loudest.

I can tell that Jacob is uncomfortable, eager to talk of loftier things.

"Who has some words of Torah to share?" he asks.

The Torah portion that week is Vayeshev, which tells the story of Joseph's dreams—the stars and the moon and the sun and the sheaves of wheat all bowing down to him. His brothers hate him for it and throw him in a pit, then sell him as a slave; they dip his coat in goat's blood and take it to their father, making him believe that his favorite son is dead. My sister's husband had been reading what the commentators had to say about these passages, specifically about the pit. Shlomo spent his days studying, for which he received a modest stipend. To make extra money, he played in a wedding band that had regular gigs around the city. He was not the most serious of yeshiva students, but it hardly mattered; his father was a scholar, his mother descended from a long line of scholars. Torah was in his blood, in his bones, suffusing all his speech.

"It says about the pit that the brothers threw Joseph in 'and the pit was empty. There was no water in it.' The great commentator Rashi asks, 'Why does the text state that the pit had no water in it? Surely, if it was empty, it did not contain water.'"

Shlomo continues. "We know that the Torah would not waste one word, not even a single letter, that every word has a purpose, placed there by God. Rashi says it like this—the pit represents the world, and the water represents Torah . . ."

As he speaks, I look at Adam, his gaze cast downward, his fingers fumbling with a breadcrumb on the tablecloth. In another city, in another life, it would have been different. In the States, Adam had trained as a lawyer; his earning potential far outweighs that of Shlomo. But in Jerusalem, it is not money or professional standing that matters, but knowledge of God's books.

Among the couples we knew, it was not uncommon for the man to spend at least the first year of marriage in yeshiva. Beginning one's marriage with Torah study created a foundation for the future. But Adam was not spending his first year of marriage studying Torah; he was working at a small law firm near the city center, while preparing for his law exams. I was working part-time as a copyeditor at the city's English-language newspaper, but did not earn enough to support us. Neither of us had rich parents, nor did we have savings to draw on.

This was the reality, which Adam knew as well as I. But still, he felt deprived. Deprived of the chance to devote himself to Torah, to master the language of the holy books and to spend his days inside them.

After I clear and wash the dishes and everyone is gone, I can feel Adam's quietness, something building up inside him.

"What's wrong?" I say and he says, "Nothing."

I ask again, and he tells me to stop asking him questions.

That night we sleep in separate beds. Not because we are fighting, but because we are commanded. Even though we are husband and wife, even though it is the Sabbath, the night on which marital relations are considered a double blessing. The reason is because I am still in the middle of my seven unclean days following menstruation. During this time, I cannot touch my husband. It's not just sex that is forbidden, but sleeping in the same bed, sitting on the same sofa, serving your husband from a platter you have eaten from.

An entire Talmudic tractate is devoted to these laws.

There is no way to reach my husband. To put my hand on his or lean my head on his shoulder or ask him to put his arms around me. Even from my bed, situated an arm's length from his, in accordance with the law, I cannot reach him.

In the winter, Jerusalem is cold. A city made of stone with no central heating, it's even colder on the Sabbath, when you can't turn on the oven or adjust the heater. But it isn't the Sabbath; it's an ordinary day of the week. Adam's parents have flown in this morning, and tonight we are meeting them for dinner. They aren't technically his parents; they are his father and new stepmother, but that's how he refers to them, as though his actual mother does not exist.

I stand in front of the mirror and try to get dressed, but I can't get dressed because I don't want to put on any of the clothes my husband expects to see me in. I'd been trying to write a poem about it, but I can't get past the first lines.

I go down to the pit of my body
The last place anyone would think to look

The truth was I could never complete a piece of writing. My drawers were filled with them—the scattered first few lines of something, scrawled on unlined paper, ripped out of a notebook, always left unfinished.

I put on a long black skirt and a dark green sweater and tie a green scarf around my head. I'd chosen the sweater because it matched my eyes. But when I look in the mirror, there is no one I can see. My sister covers her hair. My mother covers her hair.

My friends cover their hair. There was something wrong with me, something that differentiated me from other Jewish wives. Why couldn't I do what God was commanding me?

I think about what I want to wear, the kind of clothing I wore before I got married. A pair of wide-legged jeans, a wraparound sweater. But Adam did not like to see me in pants, even if they were modest. Nor did he want to see me in anything formfitting, since the shape of my body was for him alone.

Lately, it had been hard for me to get dressed, harder to leave the house. I wanted to feel happy. But how could I feel happy when I could not recognize myself?

I know that the glory of the king's daughter is within. That is what the Torah teaches, that is what God asks of us. The daughter of the king walks in modesty—that is what the prophets say. That is what I was taught in the women's seminary I attended when I'd first come to Jerusalem ten years earlier. Modesty isn't merely commanded of a Jewish woman; it is her highest calling.

Sometimes I wondered if Adam really wanted to know me or if he just wanted to know his version of me—the version that was good, the version that was modest. What he didn't want to know was that sometimes I was not good, that sometimes I was not modest.

Like the night three years earlier when I went to a party for foreign journalists with my friend Aviva from work and we met up with a journalist she knew—I knew him too since I'd met him at Aviva's apartment before—and he offered me a glass of melon-flavored vodka, and I drank it, and then I drank another one. And then I left the party early with the journalist, or maybe I left by myself, but he called me later and came over to my apartment, the one I shared with my roommate, for which I paid 400 shekels less than she did a month (because she had the bigger room, with a door that opened onto the balcony), and we started to kiss, and then he took off my dress, and then we were in my bed, and we were still kissing, and then he was doing the one thing I had told myself I would not do unless I was married, something I only realized as it was happening, happening in slow motion, without my consent but without my refusal.

The next morning, I saw the blood had stained through the sheet to the mattress.

That's the kind of thing I'm talking about, the kind of thing I could never tell Jacob.

I move in closer to the mirror to better see my flaws. The acne scars along the lower jaw, the tiny pockmarks on my cheek. There are no active eruptions, but still I am not convinced I do not need purging. I claw at my skin, at my hair, raking my nails against my flesh to extract an invisible venom. I scratch and I scratch until there is blood streaked across my face, lodged under my fingernails.

I look at the clock. It isn't late, but because it is winter, it is already dark. Soon Adam will get home from work, and it will be time to meet his father and stepmother. I go into the bathroom and shut the door. I will have to become someone my husband can recognize before he gets home.

I decide to see a therapist. Not a new therapist, but the old therapist I used to see before I got married to Adam, who preferred I not see a therapist at all. "If you have a problem," he'd told me, "you can talk to me. We can figure it out together." That's what I wanted: a husband who would listen, who would help me when I needed him. At the time, it seemed like a small thing to agree to.

Miriam is an older American expat, married to a professor at the Hebrew University. I like sitting in her office because she has a couch covered in light blue velvet that looks like the sea and a wall full of books. I tell Miriam I am crying all the time. I tell her some days I spend all day in bed, then get up to brush my teeth and prepare dinner right before Adam gets home. I tell her I cannot recognize my reflection.

"I'm afraid to do something he doesn't like," I tell her. "I'm afraid because I want to have a good marriage."

"Doing everything someone else wants—is that what you think makes a good marriage?"

I don't answer, because I have no idea what makes a good marriage.

"When you silently acquiesce to all of your spouse's desires, it breeds resentment," she says. "Doing whatever you think your spouse wants is not love."

"Then what is?"

"Your job in a marriage is to state your views and opinions and then negotiate to find a compromise."

"But what if we can't compromise?"

"When you have a different desire from your spouse," she says, "and you make it known, but then you do it anyway—*that* is love."

That night, I tell Adam I need to talk to him.

"I can't do this anymore," I say.

"Can't do what?" he says.

"Walk around like I'm a religious wife," I say.

"But you are a religious wife," he says.

"I know," I say, but I don't know what to say next.

"What are you talking about?" he says.

"Wearing long skirts, covering my hair all the time," I say. "It feels like a costume."

"But how can it be a costume if that's who you are? You want to go out in tight jeans, with everything hanging out? Don't you see that's a costume too?"

My mind starts swimming, my limbs go numb. He loves to poke holes in my arguments.

"Can you just listen to what I'm saying?"

"How can I listen if what you're saying doesn't make sense?"

I try to explain that just because it doesn't make sense to him does not mean it does not make sense. I try to explain to him that I am struggling. I try to explain that my struggle is part of my relationship with God. But Adam doesn't want to hear about this struggle or any other.

I can still remember the single time I'd tried to talk to him about the things that happened in my childhood. It was a Sabbath afternoon at the end of winter, just before spring, and we were sitting on my bed, which was technically forbidden.

"But you're okay now?" he'd said.

"Yes," I said.

"It's in the past," he said, more like a statement than a question.

"Yes," I said.

This was while we were still dating, before we were engaged, before we were married, before I realized he didn't want to know.

"Look," he says to me now. "You need to compromise."

"I'm trying to compromise," I say.

"Marriage is about becoming one," he says. "But you wouldn't know anything about that."

Soon after, I call my mother to tell her the truth. That my marriage is not working. I am trying and trying, but it is not working.

We've been on the phone for nearly an hour when my father picks up.

"Can you tell your father what's going on?" my mother says, and for some reason, I agree.

Over the course of the past ten years, my parents' marriage had somehow settled into an amiable routine—my father was still my father, muttering under his breath when he was stressed and losing his temper from time to time, but there was an ease between my parents that had not been there when I was a child. I was grateful for it, even if I could not explain it. Even my father's congregation seemed to be thriving, having recently completed renovations on a new building, with a new sanctuary named after its generous donor. Maybe after all this time, my parents' story would have a happy ending, I thought, even if it seemed like mine wouldn't.

"Adam and I are fighting all the time," I say. "We can't stop fighting."

By then, my father had married hundreds of couples, many of whom then turned to him for help. He has a gentle way of speaking, of listening without judgment. By then, he'd been counseling newly married couples for decades.

"The problem in the marriage is not that you disagree," my father tells me. "The problem is the mechanism that leads you to fight. These two things can be separated," he says. "Once the fighting subsides, you can see your differences more dispassionately."

He talks about *ahava* and *yirah*, love and fear. "The two are linked together," he tells me, as though I don't know. Everybody knows the question asked by the Talmud: What is the difference between one who performs the commandments out of love and one who performs them out of fear?

"You cannot view your life from the perspective of fear," my father says, and I know that he is right.

I think about the single time that Adam and I visited my parents' home, this past spring for Passover. As soon as we arrived, my mother put Adam to work—repairing the kitchen chairs' caning, replacing the broken light fixtures, rewiring them so they would finally be functional. I think about how happy I was to have a husband who could fix things. How happy I was to be someone's wife instead of someone's daughter.

I realize that if this marriage fails, I will not just be disappointing myself, but my mother, my father, my sister, my brothers, my aunts, my uncles, and all of my father's congregants, who had sent generous checks and purchased everything off our registry, so eager to partake in the rabbi's daughter's happiness.

The poor congregants—no one ever told them anything. They had no way of knowing how difficult it would be for this rabbi's daughter to find happiness. But I knew.

Spring was coming and, with it, the festival of Purim. The day we're commanded to dress up and give gifts to the poor, the day we're commanded to drink until we cannot tell the difference between Mordechai and Haman—the man who tried to save us, and the man who tried to kill us.

Unlike the solemn celebrations throughout the Jewish calendar, this one is joyful, marked not by adherence to a specific set of laws but by a temporary suspension of all laws. On the day of the festival, parties can be heard in every neighborhood throughout the city, on every street corner. Every year, the shops fill with three-sided poppy- and jam-filled pastries, and the streets fill with revelers drinking wine, spilling out of synagogues, disguised as kings and queens.

The past few months had been difficult. I had recently stopped covering my hair, a decision my husband did not approve of, and which led to many arguments. But I was determined to have fun on Purim. In preparation for the holiday, I'd gone to the city center and purchased a long, peroxide-blond wig, a tube of red lipstick, and a rhinestone-encrusted headband. From the back of my closet, I'd selected a formfitting black top, a pair of high-heeled boots, and a red skirt that just reached my knees.

On the day of the festival, Adam has no interest in attending a party full of drunk people, so from our apartment we depart for the Old City on foot. We take the small streets behind the old train tracks, making our way down through the Hinnom Valley, up the sloped, stone pathway that leads to the Jaffa Gate. On our way, we stop at a small *makolet* and buy a bottle of wine.

Adam does not typically drink, but it is Purim, and drinking is commanded. Still, you cannot drink wine on an empty stomach, so we look around for somewhere to eat. There is only one pizza place open, so we order two slices and sit down. Adam takes out the pocketknife he always keeps on his person, opens the bottle of wine, and fills both our cups.

"*L'chaim*," he says.

"*L'chaim*," I say, and we drink.

As we do, I toss my blond hair over one shoulder.

"The wig suits you," my husband says.

"Thanks," I say, and smile.

"Maybe you should wear one every day."

I tell him I can't believe he is bringing this up again.

"You're just doing this to upset me," he says.

"Is that what you think?"

"I understand that it's difficult for you," he says. "But you can't just act unilaterally. Marriage is about compromise. Why don't you know that?"

A few teenagers trickle into the pizza shop, young men in capes and masks.

The wine sloshes around my brain, coating everything in a greasy film. I look at Adam's face. Of all the men in the world, how did I choose him?

I once thought he was a kind man, a calm man, a man searching for holiness. He had an ascetic quality I did not share but thought that I could emulate. He was a lawyer like my uncles, like the man my father should have been, a man who could protect me. But now I could only see his inability to listen, to tolerate any position other than his own. His arrogance to think that, just because he'd discovered God, he could tell me what to do.

"You think you have a monopoly on knowing what God wants?" I scream. I don't care if anyone can hear. "You think you can speak for God?"

"You're just raising your voice so other people will hear you," he whispers. "So that you sound like you're in the right, so that you can embarrass me even more than you already have."

I push back my chair, knocking over my plastic cup of wine, and run out of the restaurant. I run through the alleyways, in my high-heeled boots and red lipstick and long blond wig, the candy-floss strands sticking to my face. I run and I run, past the old men drinking muddy coffee outside their shops, past the ultra-Orthodox mothers pushing double strollers through the narrow stone streets, trailed by children wearing crowns and carrying scepters. I run and I run, through the Hinnom Valley and past the old train tracks. I run and I run until I can't run anymore. By the time I get home, I understand.

Adam wanted a woman who followed all of God's rules, but I had never wanted to be a woman who followed all of God's rules. I wanted to be a woman who knew God.

After two years and nine months of marriage, Adam and I attend our appointment at the Jerusalem rabbinical court. My mother sits silently on a plastic chair in the waiting room with a frozen expression. My sister stands crying in the corridor, her red kerchief askew. My husband walks in and out of rooms with the scribe, who will write it all down: the daughter of, the son of, from the house of.

When the time comes, we stand before the three rabbis and the witnesses who have come to bear witness. One of the rabbis has the face of a dog, which, according to tradition, means it must be the days leading up to the Messiah. My husband holds out a piece of paper, and I cup my hands to receive it. This is the *get*, the writ of divorce. I put it in my bag, then walk to the door, then back to the table, where I take it out of my bag, in accordance with the law.

I can feel my husband's gaze. I can see his lower lip tremble, just as it had on our wedding day. I can feel my own trembling, but it is already too late.

I walk out of the court and make my way to the bench in the square where the homeless people live and the crazy people gather. From under my gray wool sweater, tears of sweat pour out of my body, and the sun lights the whole city on fire. I see the man who until that morning had been my husband walk past me. And I think, *Everything since I was born has led me to this.*

9

THE DEAD SEA

WE ARE EATING LUNCH TOGETHER as a family on a Saturday afternoon. It is almost winter. My mother is at one end of the table, the rest of us packed into folding chairs on either side. My father is not here. He is at home in Chicago, leading services at his congregation, just as he always has. But the rest of us are here, in Jerusalem, the place we have prayed to all our lives. My mother's laid out a feast—fish and cheese and olives and challah from the market, all of which we bless in due course.

It is, of course, the Sabbath.

In Jerusalem, the week revolves around the Sabbath. In Jerusalem, the whole world revolves around the Sabbath.

Rachel is still married, with a two-year-old daughter and a husband still learning in yeshiva. My three brothers are also studying in yeshiva, forswearing college and girls and whatever else American boys their age do, to immerse themselves in Torah. As for me, just months ago, I'd been a married woman with a home and two sets of dishes and two sets of bed linens of my own. The marriage had been so brief, it sometimes seemed like it never really happened, or that if it had, it had only happened in a dream.

My mother's rented apartment is in the city center, next to the record stores and travel agencies on Shamai Street, named for the great rabbinic sage. Throughout the Talmud, Shamai represents the minority opinion, the counterargument, the voice that's overruled. One street over is Hillel Street, named for the rabbinic sage whose legal opinions we follow to this day. It is a small apartment, modestly furnished in the manner of a holiday rental, with brown glass plates in the cupboards, an electric kettle, and a washing machine in the bathroom.

In Jerusalem, one is focused only on the essence of things, the things that cannot be quantified by earthly measure—the quality and focus of one's prayer, the scrupulousness with which one observes the Sabbath, the ability to see God's hand in all things.

My brothers were in Jerusalem because it was the only place in the world where Torah was everywhere. In Jerusalem, there is a yeshiva on every corner. Every yeshiva has its own character, just as every human being has their own soul. The yeshiva Joseph and Ephraim attended catered to foreign students and was known for its mystical leanings. Its students were encouraged not merely to study Talmud, but to wake before sunrise and immerse in an ice-cold mikveh (ritual bath) to purify themselves before the morning prayers.

Sometimes people go looking for God because they have no mother or father. What about us? We had a mother and a father, but our father had hurt us, and our mother had not protected us. We had a mother and a father, but still we felt like wanderers. That is where God comes in. In the Torah, God is referred to as the Creator ("And He saw that He had created the heavens and earth, and it was good"). Other times, God is referred to as a judge ("Will the judge of all the Earth not do justice?"). But there was another way to see God—and that was as a father. What were we, after all, if not children in search of a father? A father who loves his children more than anything else in the whole world.

We sit at the table in my mother's rented apartment for a long time, even after we finish eating, even after we sing the Sabbath songs of praise, even after the Grace After Meals. There is a comfort in being together we do not want to let go of, all of us together, without any threat.

My brothers and sister and I move together like a school of fish, a flock of sheep. Where one of us goes, the others follow. The God of one of us was the God of all of us. We were different—I was the bookish one, my sister the athletic one, Joseph the funniest, Ephraim the smartest, Noam the tallest and most musical—but we were also the same. We were in search of an earthly haven, a place we could feel safe.

We sit at the table talking and laughing in a way only we can understand until the air outside begins to cool and the sky begins to darken, and it's time for my brothers to rush to synagogue for the evening prayers.

You might think my parents' children fled to Jerusalem to escape our father, but that would be only part of the story.

When I left my parents' house, I left my brothers alone. When I left my parents' house, I could no longer protect my brothers from my father or from anyone else who might want to hurt them. Which begs the question—who would want to hurt them?

It had been my mother's idea, soon after I left home, to take my youngest brothers out of the community Jewish day school we'd all attended—where boys and girls prayed together in the same chapel, where girls were permitted to chant aloud from the Torah scroll, where secular knowledge was extolled—and enroll them in an Orthodox yeshiva. By then, my mother knew the kind of man my father was. She knew my brothers needed nurturing, that they needed positive male role models who could show them what a Jewish man was supposed to be. She wanted to give them their birthright—the living words of Torah—but that was not all. Perhaps at yeshiva, she hoped, a rabbi might take the place of a father.

In the summer of 1996, my brother Ephraim was a twelve-year-old boy preparing to enter eighth grade at his new Orthodox school. In preparation, it was recommended he brush up on his Talmud skills, the most essential component of a *frum* boy's curriculum. It was bad enough that we lived outside the Orthodox community, that my mother did not cover her hair with a wig, that my father was the head of a congregation where men and women sat together in the sanctuary; it would be a shame for Ephraim to lag behind in Talmud as well.

And so, that summer, he began lessons with Rabbi Gottlieb, a teacher at the school who tutored on the side. The rabbi was a respected Torah scholar, with a trimmed beard and a receding hairline. He had a wife and eight children. My brother learned one-on-one with him the whole summer.

From the beginning, this rabbi saw how quickly Ephraim's mind worked. From the beginning, he told my mother how brilliant Ephraim was.

If there are five children, who can you say is the middle child? I was the oldest—"our eldest," my father used to say, hands on my shoulders, a smile forming on his lips. Rachel was the youngest girl. Next was Joseph, which made him the oldest boy. Noam was the baby, so that left Ephraim. His baby shoes were the only ones that were never bronzed, his bar mitzvah the only one that wasn't photographed.

Once school began, this rabbi took Ephraim under his wing, as he did so many of the boys. He was more than a teacher. He was a rebbe in the old-school manner, like the rebbes in the Torah academies of Eastern Europe in the eighteenth and nineteenth centuries—a teacher, yes, but more important, a confidant, a mentor, a friend. He was Ephraim's teacher for many years. After that, he was Noam's teacher too.

Rabbi Gottlieb was the rebbe the boys could talk to, the one who told his students they could ask him anything, no subject was off-limits—even if it was about their changing bodies, or a question about something so personal and private you might not have words for it; they could come to him with those too. He was even willing to talk about pornography with them; there was no need to be ashamed, he told them, no reason to feel embarrassed. His students called him "Rebs," a term of endearment that was short for *rebbe*.

Rabbi Gottlieb quickly became my brother's favorite teacher, which was no surprise. He was everybody's favorite teacher. Even my father, who seemed to respect nobody, admired him. How could he not? The man was a *Talmid Chacham*, a scholar.

Rabbi Gottlieb had his students over to his house all the time. He bought them pizza and Coca-Cola.

He played racquetball at the Jewish Community Center with them, then undressed and joined them in the shower.

It was okay, he told them, when he showed them his *aver*, using the Talmudic terminology.

With most of the students, it stopped there. But with other students, it went further. For some children, it was worse, because for some children it is always worse.

One Friday afternoon, just after the last class, only a few hours before Shabbos, this rabbi waited by the door for one of his students, one of his favorite students, a student whom he loved. This boy was from a scholarship family—his father worked in heating and air-conditioning installation, his brother had behavioral problems, his parents were in the midst of a contentious divorce. The rabbi waited by the door for this boy, asked him to stay back. And when he did, he placed this boy's hand on his penis.

This boy and his parents were cautioned by the rabbis not to speak out, not to press charges. Life is difficult enough, and what damage was really done? And so they agreed.

This is just one story. What about the other stories? To tell each one would take a lifetime.

When my mother got the call informing her that her son's favorite teacher was a child abuser, she did not believe it. Of course she did not believe it. She called and left a message on his answering machine, offering her support. But the following night, a meeting for parents was held at the school.

"Some kids will talk about it, some won't," a psychologist told the parents.

Ephraim would not talk. Neither would Noam.

My brothers said they had not been directly affected, but beyond that, they said nothing.

Because the boys who had been assaulted were not from prominent families, nothing was done. This rabbi, no less than a long line of priests and youth group leaders before him, was not stupid. Like any predator bearing God's word, this rabbi was a master at his craft. He'd targeted the boys from broken families—families in which the parents were divorced or there were too many kids or not enough money or all of the above. The kids whose parents were already drowning.

What if I told you that, one day, I would hear a story like this about my father? A story where there is a rabbi, and there is a student, and the student is a child. A story that surprises me, even though I've been surprised before. If I told you that story, would you believe me? Or would you say, Why ruin a man's life? I know this rabbi, and he is a good man.

For the religious Jewish community, there had always been a simple taxonomy—the men, who deserve to be protected, and the children, who don't. Men, who deserve to be believed, and children, whom no one should believe.

This was not Rabbi Gottlieb's first offense. He had, like so many men of faith before him, simply been moved from school to school, city to city, without a single word of warning or apprehension. There was no need to speak *lashon harah* about a beloved teacher, a man who had given so much to so many. No need to jeopardize his *parnasa*, his ability to provide for his family. No need to bring shame to a man who, even if he had been guilty of an indiscretion or two, had already repented.

If you're wondering what happened to this rabbi, you should know he was protected.

Protected so that he never went to jail. Protected so that the story was kept out of major newspapers, so that no shame came to the community. The only repercussion that befell him was that he was forced to resign from his teaching position and barred from taking any other teaching positions in the future. Yet he was still permitted—by ordinance of the *beis din*, the religious court—to attend local synagogues, though only on the Sabbath, when presumably his evil inclinations might be suspended.

Periodically, there were sightings of "Rebs," as my brother and his friends still referred to him, even after everything happened. One kid said they saw him at Hollywood Video. Someone else said they saw him at a fish restaurant. Someone else said they had seen him delivering mail. For a time, there was a rumor circulating among my brother's friends that he was working as a cable guy.

In the wake of the controversy, community leaders agreed that the matter should be kept quiet. Members of the community were reminded that the rabbi had daughters of marriageable age, whose *shidduchim* should not be placed in jeopardy. The head of the *beis din* declared it would be a *shanda*, or disgrace, if word got out.

The Jewish people do not want interference in their affairs unless it is from God. God knows the Jewish people have suffered enough, that we have been persecuted in every generation from the beginning of time—the scapegoat, the Satan, the Christ killer. What do the goyim say about the Jews? That we are tricksters, parasites, bloodsuckers. That we kill Christian children and drink their blood at the Seder table.

The gentiles hate the Jews anyway, why give them another reason?

I was an adult when the story broke—a twenty-five-year-old woman, not yet engaged, living in the holiest city in the world, as far away from my family as I could get. I only heard about these events after the fact, which is to say after the facts, once so hidden, had made themselves known. My mother called to tell me over the phone one night, which was only night for me since we lived in different hemispheres.

When my mother told me these facts over the phone, the anger I felt was of a weight and dimension previously unknown to me.

I thought, *It's a good thing I live half a world away because if I didn't, I would find this man and kill him.*

I thought, *I could kill this man with my bare hands.*

I thought, *It's not enough that I spent my whole life trying to protect my brothers from my father and failing. I'd failed to protect them from this man too.*

In the western part of Jerusalem, the streets are silent on the Sabbath, the shops and eateries closed. But on the weekdays, Jerusalem takes on the contours of an ordinary city. The buses run, the produce vendors hawk their wares in the covered market, the one-legged beggars cluster around the Central Bus Station, offering blessings in exchange for money. While my brothers are studying Torah in yeshiva, on the premise that this knowledge will bring them closer to God—no, on the premise that this knowledge *is* closeness to God—I am still working as a copyeditor at the city's English-language newspaper, a job I have held for too long.

Since I left my husband's home, I have no place to live. My copyeditor's salary is not enough for me to rent an apartment on my own, and I cannot imagine going back to live with a roommate. For a time after my divorce, I stayed with my sister and her husband on a cot in the baby's room, then at a friend's empty apartment while they were visiting family abroad. But now my mother is here on an extended visit, and I am living with her in her rental apartment, as though I am a child.

Sometimes I am asked to work the night shift in the newsroom, where I edit stories being reported in real time. There is no shortage of these stories. Shootings and bombings and demolitions, protests and counterprotests, assassinations, retaliations, factions and extreme factions, factions within factions within factions, extrajudicial killings. On and on and on in a never-ending loop, everyone believing they are right, everyone ready to die to prove how much they love God.

More often, I work the day shift, editing the softer pieces, the profiles and gallery openings, the book pages and advertorials. I like thinking about the words and sentence structure and comma placement rather than the horrors that crowd my nightmares, which I am powerless to staunch. Not long ago I was offered a position as the editor of the weekend magazine, but I refused it, just as I'd refused every opportunity I'd been offered. I want to stay in the shadows, where no one can see me, where I can quietly tell myself I am a prolific poet or a great novelist, despite never having published anything aside from a handful of articles for the local Friday supplement—most recently, about a group of secular activists protesting the building of an Orthodox synagogue in their neighborhood—but those didn't really count.

After work, I walk the long way home through the souk, stopping to buy bags of cucumbers and tomatoes, the air salty from the open tubs of olives swimming in brine, the air briny where the fish lie gutted on small mounds of crushed ice. I walk past the pizza shop that was blown apart and quickly rebuilt so that people could try to pretend that nothing had happened, that nothing was still happening. I keep walking until I reach my mother's apartment, where I sleep in a small bedroom the size of a closet.

In Jerusalem, a woman without a husband is barely a woman. In Jerusalem, a woman without children is not a woman at all.

Often when I return home from work, my mother has dinner waiting for me. Even if it is just some sliced bread and a chopped salad. I am an adult, but I need someone to take care of me.

⌒

At Noam's yeshiva, boys are dying. One evening when I get home from work, my brother comes over to my mother's apartment, and right away, I can see something is wrong, his eyes are hollowed and bloodshot. His blood is my blood; I could always feel what my sister and brothers were feeling more than I could feel anything else. He is standing, then pacing, too agitated to sit down.

"What happened?" I say.

"A kid died today," he says.

"What kid?" I say.

The kid's name was Micah, he was from LA. Two nights ago, he had traveled with two friends from Jerusalem to Lod to buy heroin. They'd come back blasted, Noam told me, falling over, their eyes—Noam had no words for what their eyes looked like. Micah had mixed the heroin with Xanax, then with more heroin. He was out of it, he told his friends, he needed to go to sleep. But before he did, he told Noam to wake him up the next morning; he wanted to make sure he didn't miss *shiur*, the morning Talmud lesson.

It's not like Micah was the only kid in the yeshiva doing drugs. The guys from Queens and Brooklyn were taking tons of Xanax. One kid had fallen out of a third-story window.

The yeshiva Noam was studying at was known as a yeshiva for troubled boys. Boys from religious homes in New York and LA and Baltimore and Dallas—but not the right homes.

These were not the sons of doctors and lawyers and businessmen, but the sons of the Jews you never hear about, the bakery workers and part-time repairmen, the poor Jews no one likes to talk about. The boys were troubled—by drugs or by rage or by something else their parents couldn't understand. These parents sent their sons to Jerusalem, hoping Torah would turn their lives around. What these parents didn't understand was that it was Torah that had ruined them in the first place.

I didn't really understand why Noam had chosen to go there. At the time, I still didn't know the scope of what my brothers had witnessed.

How does a young man of seventeen or eighteen come to find himself at a yeshiva for troubled boys? Many years later, I would learn there was a familiar trajectory. A family without means, a family of many children, a boy yearning for someone to pay attention to him. Micah from LA, Benny from Queens, Yossi from Baltimore—every kid had the same story, Noam would tell me many years later. A rabbi who molested kids, never went to jail, then stayed in the community.

A religious Jewish boy who has been brought up to fear God and the Torah, to respect his teachers, his rabbis, his parents, his aunts, his uncles, the elders of his synagogue, a boy like this would never think to question the behavior of a beloved rebbe. And even if he did, who would believe him? Belief is a slippery thing; unlike ritual or law, it cannot be commanded. People like to talk about the virtue of belief, but only when it's about something they believe in. When they choose not to believe, they make that a virtue too.

When you are a religious boy, you are told you're a member of the chosen people, but what happens when you speak about what's happened to you? Then you are not chosen, you are not loved.

Micah's room was right across the hallway from Noam's, and it was Noam and a few of their friends who found him the next morning, his body stiff, his skin blue. Many years later, Noam would tell me it wasn't like a body; it was like a stone.

They ran down the hallway to get a rabbi, and when they told him what had happened, the rabbi started crying.

It is only many years later, when Noam's own life is in danger, when I stay up all night with him trying to understand everything that's happened, that he will explain all this to me. I will rush to write down every word he is saying, because every word he is saying contains universes.

But, on this day, my brother doesn't tell me anything. My mother has brought out a bowl of chopped salad and a plate of sliced bread and canned fish. But my brother is not hungry. He says he has to get back to yeshiva. He picks up his things, his headphones and guitar, the two things he always has with him, and without saying goodbye, walks back into the Jerusalem night.

My mother has already been in Jerusalem for a month when my father comes to join her. Usually when my mother comes to visit her children in Jerusalem, she comes alone, but this time their eldest daughter has just gone through a divorce and their youngest son has just witnessed a death, so my father comes too. Perhaps he can feel that we need him. Perhaps he feels he can comfort us.

The night my father arrives, he takes us out for dinner to an American-style burger place in the German Colony and tells us to order whatever we want. In Jerusalem, nearly all the restaurants are kosher, and my father has always loved to spoil us.

A few days later, we take a trip to the Dead Sea, a body of water so rich in minerals, nothing can live in it. People come to the Dead Sea from all over the world to soak in its healing waters, to cover themselves with mud from its shores. We squeeze ourselves into the small rental car for the drive down to the sea, my father at the wheel.

We are packed like sardines for the hour-long drive, Joseph sitting on Noam's lap and Rachel sitting on mine. The Dead Sea is situated 1,300 feet below sea level; we are traveling to the lowest place on earth. I don't think any of us are wearing seat belts.

"It's a good thing I remembered my Novocain," I say, and my mother laughs.

I can still remember the precipitous, craggy descent along the single curving road, the way my ears popped as we descended lower and lower and lower.

It is winter, and it is cold, the sky white and gray. It is too cold to go to the beach, so we go instead to a spa nestled in the foothills where the biblical David once fled to escape King Saul's fury. It isn't really a spa at all, but a Soviet-style bathhouse with separate sections for men and for women, where, for twenty-five shekels, you are given a key to a small metal locker to keep your clothes in while you join the uninhibited bathers soaking in the spa's indoor sulfur and salt pools.

I am in the salt pool with my mother and sister on the women's side, so I do not know what happened. All I know is that when we finally emerge from the women's locker room, wet-haired and red-faced, we find my brothers in the overcast solarium, their eyes defeated.

"What happened?" I ask, but they won't say.

Something about Dad, who has gone missing.

We wait all afternoon in the solarium for him to appear. We can't leave without him because he has the keys to the car. When he finally emerges, soon before sundown, he is enraged. The silent, furtive kind of rage necessitated by a public setting. My father was always angry about something, but he would never tell you the reason. As usual, someone has wronged him, but he won't say who. As usual, he is furious with one of my brothers, but he won't say why.

We are in the desert, and the air is getting colder. Night is falling. We have no choice. We have to get back to Jerusalem, and so we pile back into the car, this time in silence; no one wants to talk. For a moment, I think we will spend the ride in silence, but that changes when we pull onto the single curving road leading away from the sea and the crystalline salt formations dotting the coastline.

As we begin our ascent to Jerusalem, the steep sandstone cliffs rising up on either side, my father accelerates. He doesn't just accelerate, he floors it. He is not just exceeding the speed limit; he is trying to see how fast a car can go. Not just this car, but any car. Every time we hit a sharp curve, he speeds up.

We are all sitting in the back seat, one on top of the other. We begin to scream. We begin to cry. We scream for him to stop. But he doesn't stop.

I can feel a cramped, frozen feeling in my legs, my body bracing itself for what is coming.

The car rushing toward the edge.

The car rushing toward the abyss.

Everyone knows you can't get out of a speeding car, which means we are trapped. The salty waters, with their healing minerals, lie below us, while God sits above us, looking down from his throne.

I think, not for the first or the last time, that my father is trying to kill us.

God,
Are you listening?
God,
Can you hear us?

In ancient Jerusalem, when the Holy Temple still stood, the Jewish people were commanded by God to bring sacrifices. There were many types of sacrifices. Offerings of goats and sheep, wheat and barley. Libations of wine. Incense made of myrrh and frankincense. Sacrifices brought as an act of thanksgiving, of atonement, of regret. All burned on an altar to God.

Unlike their pagan counterparts, the ancient Israelites did not practice child sacrifice. The biblical God had forbidden it. The prophets Jeremiah and Isaiah railed against it—the practice of burning one's child alive to pacify Moloch. It was one of the things that separated the Jewish God from the other gods—the belief that there is nothing more sacred than a human life, that every human being is created in God's image.

In the end, my father did not kill us. Not on that night and not on any of the nights that followed. Instead, we kept on living. In the coming years, some of us would move back to America, some of us would leave God behind, some of us would be so angry, we would try to set ourselves on fire. Among the five of us, we would get engaged, married, divorced, and married again. Among the five of us, we would give birth to a son, a daughter, then another daughter, then another daughter, a set of twins. Even when we thought more life could not come from us, it did. We had no choice. We believed in God, and God had commanded us to live.

10

SOUNDS OF JOY AND GLADNESS

CHICAGO LOOKS DIFFERENT FROM ABOVE, especially at night, when the moon turns the lake into a sheet of smoked glass. Beneath the cloud cover, the heat from the earth's surface rises, and the cool air descends. I am doing what I have done so many times since I left my parents' house at seventeen—so many times, even though I'd promised myself not to. I am flying into Chicago, the city by the lake, the city of broad shoulders, the hog butcher to the world, because my brother Ephraim is getting married.

Eight years have passed since we all lived in Jerusalem, since we all dispersed in 2005—Noam to attend music school (he soon dropped out), Joseph and his wife to the eastern shore of Canada, where Joseph had gotten a job offer, Rachel and her seven-year-old daughter to Tel Aviv, where she worked at a start-up. Of the five of us, Ephraim was the only one to return to Chicago, the only one to dare to make a life here—here in the shadow of our family's dissolution, where our house still stood without our family in it, where my father's congregation still existed without my father as its leader, where everybody in the community would still recognize our faces, even as they wondered among themselves what happened to the rabbi and the rabbi's children.

As for me, I am living a quiet life on a quiet street in Jerusalem, where palm trees keep guard like sentries. I live with my second husband, who I met at a writing workshop he was teaching. When he asked everyone to go around and name their favorite writer, I named Raymond Carver, the author of a story about a blind man trying to imagine a cathedral, its gargoyles and flying buttresses and spires. For a time, I'd carried that story collection around with me like a prayer book, which in some ways it was. After the workshop, he told me Carver was his favorite too.

His name was Jeremy, and he was American. He spent part of his time studying, part of his time writing, and the other part editing the work of a professor at the university, but the main thing he did was read. All he ever did was read. While he ate, while he drank, while he smoked. He had a hole in his jacket because he did not care about those things. He laughed a lot, but he also seemed sad, which explained why I could talk to him.

Like me, Jeremy had once scrupulously observed the laws of the Sabbath and kashrut, but no longer did. We were trying to be writers, but in the meantime, we worked as editors, polishing other people's words while dreaming of our own. On Friday afternoons, we took the bus to Tel Aviv to spend Shabbat with my sister and niece. We would walk to the beach, stopping to buy fresh pineapple juice and melon juice along the way.

So far, this marriage was going better than the first, but still it was not easy. I was not good at being alone, but I also was not good at being married—none of us were. Rachel had gotten divorced soon after me, and from what I could gather, Joseph would soon be next. I did not know Jenn, the woman Ephraim was marrying, any more than I'd known my other siblings' spouses. Maybe it was because we all lived far apart or because we knew there was no point, since all marriages are doomed to fail or because we knew we could never love anyone as much as we loved each other.

The plane ride is long, twelve hours long, and I can feel the straps of my sandals cutting into my feet, puffy from the flight. I'd decided to come in a few days early, without my husband, who'd be arriving later. I wanted the extra time to be alone with my family, but now I question my logic. I am in the first days of my last trimester, dehydrated and exhausted.

Beneath the roar of the engine, I can feel the queasiness of the plane's descent, the intermittent air pockets and changing wind patterns, the turbulence that makes it so hard to come back down to earth. I sip my carbonated beverage to steady myself. I place my hands on my round belly and feel nothing, just the turbulence inside me. I look out the window at the smoke rising up from the tarmac and realize that all the structures that once held our family in place are gone, that there is no God or architecture left to hide behind.

It is my sister who spies him first, standing outside the elevator bank on the fifth floor of the Blackstone Hotel, where we are all staying for the wedding weekend. He is wearing a military-style side cap, cocked at an angle, and a thin, well-tended mustache. I'd seen him too, but assumed he was one of the bride's foreign-born cousins, one of a dozen or more who had flown in for the wedding. It is only when I hear my sister say, "Hi, Dad," in her distant and resigned tone that I understand that the man with the mustache is, in fact, my father.

Perhaps it shouldn't have come as a surprise that he arrived in costume. My father's real self had been buried for so long it was as though it no longer existed. Now that he was not the rabbi of a congregation, he required another disguise.

It was only two years earlier that he had been unceremoniously fired from his pulpit of thirty years without cause or recompense.

Soon after, he and my mother sold their house and moved to Miami, where, with the help of my father's cousin Jerry and his well-connected wife, Eileen, he'd managed to land a plum pulpit, with a well-endowed board and a domed sanctuary overlooking the water.

For a moment, we thought this might mark a new beginning. A chance for my father to return to the beach where his parents had raised him so many years ago. But, in Florida, it took only eighteen months for my father to lose his job. After that, he lost everything.

It was around this time that my mother finally left him, left with just a small suitcase after placing a handful of valuables in a safe-deposit box in Miami. She told my father she was going to Nova Scotia to help Joseph and his wife with the new baby, which was true. But it was also true that this time she would not be coming back. She did not tell my father this because she was afraid that, this time, he might kill her.

Now we are all in the elevator, and my father is touching me gently on the shoulder, offering me a light kiss on the cheek.

"What's with the mus*tache*?" I ask him, instinctively emphasizing the second syllable.

"I thought it made me look sophisticated," he says, his lips turning up at the corners.

"It sure does," my sister says. "What are you, traveling incognito?"

"I'm trying to be inconspicuous," he says, pausing to gauge our response, "in deference to your mother. You know, I'm not sure she wants me here. I'm not sure anyone does."

We know what we are supposed to say. Of course we want you here, Dad. Everyone does. It's your son's wedding. You belong here more than anyone. But I say none of these things because I don't want him here, and it was hard to think of anyone, aside from my brother, who did.

In the weeks leading up to the wedding, my father's behavior had gotten worse. He'd begun calling my mother five, six, seven times a day, and when she didn't pick up, he began issuing threats. Sometimes she'd call and relay the threats to me:

This is your husband calling. If you do not call me back, if you cannot manage to remember your wedding vows, then I will not come to your son's wedding. Is that what you want? For your son not to have his father there? It's up to you.

"What are you going to do?" I'd asked her.

"I'm not going to give him the power to upset me."

This was how my mother had begun talking in the past year, which only made things worse.

This weekend would be the first time our father would be seeing our mother since she left him. How many times had I heard him threaten her for that very thing? *If you leave, you leave in a body bag.* Those were words I'd heard my father say since I was a child, words that had slid from my short-term memory into my long-term memory, words that had lodged themselves in my brain and never left. Words that explained why my singular purpose this weekend was to keep our father away from our mother. I'd even asked Joseph, who was here without his wife or daughters, to keep watch over her, to make sure she was not left alone, not even for a minute.

Now my sister and I are in the elevator with our father, who is inviting us up to his room.

"I've got some delicious salted macadamias," he is saying. "And some wonderful oranges—I brought them all the way from Florida."

I can see my sister's face softening, the way she is letting herself feel bad for him, which is not difficult, given the facts. My sister makes eye contact with me, silently begging me to accompany her into my father's lair.

"Sorry," I say, "I have to rest."

It was true. Before I left, my midwife had reminded me to stay hydrated, to spend as much time as possible with my feet up. But it was also true that I could not be in the same room as my father for any length of time. My sister, apparently, could take it. This was one way in which we differed—the amount we could handle without breaking.

It's the day before the wedding, and I've just gotten out of the bath. My husband has gone to see some of the city, encouraging me to take it easy. I know I am not resting as much as I should be. Even at night, I cannot sleep. I can feel the heaviness creeping into my limbs, an underwater sensation filling my head.

I was as surprised as anyone to find myself pregnant. I had never fantasized about motherhood, never dreamed of holding a baby in my arms. As a girl, I'd watched my mother, and what I'd learned was this: If you are a mother, someone will always need you. And if someone always needs you, you cannot disappear. My whole life I'd wanted to disappear, which I knew was a problem. A woman who wants to disappear has no business being a mother.

Then, last year, my husband got sick. It came out of nowhere and vanished just as quickly, but there were moments when I wondered what would remain if he were gone. I thought about all the ways I resisted life, the thin but impermeable membrane I placed between myself and other people, between myself and the divine. I thought about what my mother used to say when I was young. Every child is a gift from God. Every baby brings its own blessing.

Soon after my husband's illness, I'd gone to see a mystic who lived in a stone house surrounded by eucalypti. He did not see me in the main house, but in the small house behind the main house where he met with his petitioners. He told me the Angel of Death had been chasing me—my husband and me both. He called out to God and begged Him to release me. He prayed to our Heavenly Father, demanding my instant healing. I did not understand what was happening in that moment, but tears streamed down my face, and I could feel something shift in the heavenly order of things, something ancient being cleared out, something new called into being.

At the beginning of the pregnancy, there was vomiting. When there wasn't vomiting, there was the threat of vomiting. But that passed. And what came in its place was a strange kind of calm, a calm I'd never felt before, the kind of calm that made me think, for the first time, that maybe I could be the kind of mother I wanted to be: patient and even-tempered, grounded in myself, glowing without makeup. The kind of mother who built a life for her child where he knew he was safe, the kind of mother who would protect her child from anything.

Now I am finally doing what my midwife instructed—wrapped in a hotel robe, propped against the bed's heavily upholstered bolsters, I drink my water and place my hands on my belly.

"Hi, baby," I say, and move my hands back and forth over the rounded surface.

There's a knock on the door. When I ask who it is, my sister says, "You have to come now. There's been a breach."

"What's happening?" I say, but she will not tell me anything.

I put on some clothes and follow my sister, the click of my flip-flops echoing down the hallway, my newly pedicured feet like pontoons, the nails receding ever further into the flesh. We arrive at my mother's room, where she is lying in a king-sized bed, under the covers, overcome with laughter. My brothers are wearing their workout clothes, Joseph sitting on the bed next to my mom, Ephraim leaning up against the bathroom door, checking his phone, Noam slumped in the corner. To a man, they are quiet.

"What happened?" I demand. I can feel my rage opening up like a flower, blooming into view. I direct my gaze at Joseph, to let him know I hold him accountable.

"We were going to the hotel gym to work out, and . . . when we came back, Dad was here."

It was Joseph who had started the workout craze among my brothers years ago; now they each had their arduous routines. My brothers were strong, but they still had the frightened eyes of little boys.

"What do you mean Dad was here?" I say. "How did he get in the room? He just slithered in? Like a snake?"

"Someone must have forgotten to close the door," Ephraim says, deadpan.

"Didn't I tell you not to leave Mom alone for a second?" I say to Joseph.

Joseph likes to be good and responsible, and I almost feel bad for trying to make him feel bad, but I cannot stop. I am an adult, I remind myself. An adult woman who left her parents' home decades ago, but it doesn't matter. There is still a sense of unrealness about my own life. The only thing that has ever felt real to me is my family and how I could save them.

"Didn't I tell you?" I say to Joseph. "This isn't my job. This can't always be my job."

Joseph doesn't say anything, just keeps staring ahead. My mother is still laughing. "Mom, can you please stop? Can you just tell me what happened?"

"I was taking a nap," she says, "and all of a sudden, I look up—and there's your father! He's standing right over me! He's watching me sleep!"

Apparently, that's when Joseph came back to get his water bottle, saw our father, and told him to leave.

"But your father kept saying, 'I want to talk to you alone! I want to talk to you alone!'" my mother says, and this makes her start laughing again.

"What's so funny?" Ephraim says.

"This is ridiculous," I say. "Mom, get a hold of yourself."

"What's so funny?" Ephraim says again, but nobody answers.

"I'm going back to my room," my sister says.

Joseph is sitting on the bed next to my mom, frozen into place. Noam is already gone.

"Mom, I think you have PTSD," I tell her.

"I think you're right," she says, and this makes her laugh even harder. Her laughter fills the room. It echoes down the hallway and comes in through the vents. It fills the hotel, the city, the water along the coast. My mother's laughter fills my head, even after I return to my room, climb into bed, and try to sleep.

That night, the bride's parents host a cocktail party. My sister and I get out of the elevator, our arms linked, our fingers intertwined, as though forming a barricade, which we are. It's already warm when we arrive, the bodies of two hundred young and old

Jews packed into the red velvet-flocked underground ballroom, which, according to the plaque on the wall, had once been Al Capone's speakeasy.

We know my father is lurking about somewhere; the only question is where and how we can avoid contact. But within seconds, there he is—just steps away from the elevator, standing with my mother's two brothers, Peter and Paul, and their blond, impeccably dressed wives. Even under the best circumstances, my mother's brothers view my father with removed disdain; I can't imagine how they are faring now.

"Well, look who's here," my father says, in an unabashed display of fatherly attentiveness.

"Hi, Dad," my sister and I say at the same time, ducking our heads, wishing we could disappear.

"Hello, Rachel," he says and kisses my sister's cheek.

He leans in and grazes my ear with his lips. "Hi, chubs," he says, low enough that no one can hear.

It takes me a second to realize what is happening. I am growing a baby inside me, and my father is calling me fat. Maybe it's a joke. My mom says he intends for his words to hurt, that that is their singular and express purpose, but I am not entirely convinced. Even now. Even now, I think, he would be kind if he knew how. He would be kind if it hadn't gotten beaten out of him. He would be kind if his brain weren't a nuclear-waste site leaking hazardous runoff. There is still a part of me that believes no one is more shocked by the words that come out of his mouth than he is, that he would take them all back, if he could.

I mumble something about needing a glass of water.

"We'll see you soon!" my sister waves as we head for the bar. It is not easy navigating our way among all the guests, most of whom are from Jenn's side, since her parents are paying for everything.

Finally, we reach the bar, where my sister orders a whiskey for herself and a club soda for me.

From our perch, we can see our father deeply engaged in conversation with the bride's South African cousins.

"You know, I have a special place in my heart for Afrikaans," he is saying. Soon he will be busting out key phrases, claiming fluency.

Just then we spot our baby brother, who has shown up in his uniform: black pants, an unbuttoned black shirt, two gold chains around his neck, and rose-tinted glasses, which may or may not be intended as a joke.

"Noam!" my sister calls out.

Noam had been living in LA for a few years by then, in an apartment with his bandmate in Culver City. Noam played guitar, wrote the songs, and sang them. They'd recorded an album, but nothing really happened with it, and then they started fighting. Then my brother's bandmate asked him to move out; his father owned the building, so it was his right. What it meant for my brother was that he had no place to live.

Noam saunters over to us, slowly, to prove he's not in any rush.

"Hey," he says. "What's up?"

I look at my baby brother, and I can see he is a man, or at least that he wishes he were.

"Where are these from?" I ask, gently fingering the chains around his neck.

"They were a birthday present from my girlfriend."

"Val?" I say, and I wonder why he says "girlfriend," as though we don't know her name.

"Yeah."

"Wow, that's a really nice present," I say, but I can tell it comes out wrong.

"I mean, it's not like they're real," he says, and I wish I hadn't said anything.

"Look who it is," a familiar voice says. It's Nate, one of Ephraim's oldest friends. He too has stayed in Chicago, where his family's real estate business is located. He is like any number of the nice Jewish boys my brothers grew up with—born into wealth, protected from harm, his life set out before him. Soon he is showing us pictures on his phone—of his beautiful house, of his beautiful wife, a kid on the way.

"What are you up to, man?" Nate asks my brother. "Where you living these days?"

"You know, here and there—anywhere people let me stay."

Nate laughs. "No, seriously, man, where you at?"

"I am being serious," Noam says, and Nate's smile fades out.

"How old are you now?" he says, and I can feel every hair on Noam's body bristle.

"Fuck you," Noam says. "Fuck you and your fancy house."

"Noam!" my sister says.

"Hey, man, I'm not trying to get down on you," Nate starts to say, but Noam is already gone.

I wait for my sister's witty retort, but there is none. I look at her face, and I can see it is collapsing.

"Excuse us," I say. I grab her hand, and we make it to the bathroom just as the tears begin to roll down her face, when the door bursts open and a gaggle of Jenn's Israeli cousins come in— teetering in metallic, high-heeled sandals, smelling of cigarettes and perfume bought at discount at the duty-free shop. I push past them, holding my sister's hand as she trails behind me. We go upstairs and traipse across the lobby to a smaller bathroom I'd used earlier. When you're pregnant, you know where all the bathrooms are. It is here, inside an old-fashioned, single-stall affair, that my sister starts sobbing. I hold her, and she lets herself grow heavy against me.

My sister is never the one who loses it; that has always been my job. I can still remember the Sabbath afternoons when I was ten and she was seven, or maybe I was eleven and she was eight, and there was a blowout—that was the word I used for it then, the word I wrote in purple marker in my diary—and I stayed for it, stayed in the house, where I jumped up and down between my parents, where I made such a scene that my father had no choice but to turn his attention away from my mother, and turn toward me. My sister never stayed; she would never stay if she could help it. She was always off on her bike, on her way to the playground, out circling the block.

"What is it?" I ask her now, but all she can do is cry.

"What happened to Noam?" she finally says. "Where did he go?"

The bar is closing up, and the guests are beginning to disperse, but the night is not over until we do the rehearsal—a pre-enactment of the movements we will make tomorrow, a foreshadowing of our own actions. My father is eager to participate—relishing the role he's been assigned, as though in a play. I know my father so well, better than I know myself, better than I know anything. There are no cousins here; it's just the immediate families. And what is more immediate than my father's need to be near my mother, now that they are finally being acknowledged for the family that they are?

I can see him moving toward her, edging imperceptibly ever closer, as though his intentions are benevolent, as though all he wants is closeness.

I go over and whisper to Mick, who will be playing guitar during the procession, "Go put your arm around my mom."

Mick is Ephraim's best friend, so I can treat him like a brother. He does as I say, and, instantly, his arm around my mother's shoulders calms me, but I can see my father's teeth set against each other, his jaw locked into place.

"Okay," Jenn is saying, the pitch of her voice rising, as she may or may not be drunk, "we need all the siblings here. *All* the siblings. Is everyone here?"

By now, I am seated, my suede wedges removed, my feet resting on a chair.

"Where's Noam?" Jenn asks Ephraim, as though he would know, as though he's his brother's keeper.

"I'll find him," Ephraim says, and before anyone realizes what's happening, he is bounding up the turned mahogany staircase two steps at a time, disappearing out of view. Because he is my brother, I can feel the impulse to harm moving through him, giving him energy, gathering speed. He wants to let Noam know how much he has hurt him, but words will not suffice; he will need to hit him. I knew how his body works because it's our inheritance.

My siblings and I were not violent people, but we were people who could be violent. It was the river that ran through us. We tried to help it, but sometimes we couldn't help it. We had learned from our father, who had learned from his father.

I leave my shoes on the floor and race up the stairs after my brother. I do a 360-degree scan of the red-carpeted room, my eyes trained for movement. Out of the corner of my eye, I see Ephraim darting across the crimson expanse; he's moving fast, but I manage to grab his arm as he makes his way for the door.

"I'm so fucking sick of this," he says.

I am afraid of what Ephraim could do to Noam. I am afraid of what Noam could do to Ephraim. I am afraid of what Ephraim could do to himself.

"Sit down with me for a minute," I tell him, knowing I can calm someone else in a way I can never calm myself. But he has already wrestled free of me, already propelled himself out the door and into the night. He will be getting married the next day, which brings its own delusions to light—namely, that people will be happy for you just because you want them to be.

The wedding is held at an art museum with soaring ceilings and glass walls. Sculptural arrangements of yellow calla lilies and fiddlehead ferns adorn a sea of tables surrounding a white dance floor, visible from the mezzanine, where the ceremony will take place. The bride sits proudly on the bridal chair, flanked by her mother and my mother, by the sisters and aunts. A long stretch of women waits in line to give her a kiss and squeeze her hand. Jenn is older than my brother by several years—nearly my age—and I can feel how long she's waited for this day.

I get up from my seat and slip away to the room where the men are. Ephraim was not religious anymore; with the exception of Joseph, none of us were. But on his wedding day, as on all our wedding days, we follow the ancient choreography.

Ephraim holds court at the center of a long table, the men singing and pounding on the table with their fists, glasses of scotch continuously refilled. To his left sits Jenn's father, a biblical scholar with half a dozen books to his name and an endowed chair at a Midwestern university. To his right is my father, who no longer has a congregation or a wife or money or children who speak to him with any regularity, but today he has this: he is the groom's father, a necessary figure in the celebration. Gone was the ridiculous hat and absurd mustache, and in their place were an expensive dark suit, a large velvet kippah, and the veneer of piety—as though he'd gone back in time to retrieve the person we'd once believed him to be.

On the day of his wedding, it is customary for the groom to give over words of Torah to show that he is a scholar worthy of his bride. It is also customary that the wedding guests do everything they can to interrupt him, so as not to shame a less learned groom. This was not the case for my brother, whose brain, like my father's, could expand to take in an infinite amount of information. Ephraim worked in customer service at a small software company, but his real passion was knowledge, any kind of knowledge. Having mastered the Five Books of Moses and the seventy-two Talmudic tractates, he also possessed an exhaustive knowledge of early American history and twentieth-century literature. The only dream I ever heard him talk about was being a contestant on a trivia game show, so he could finally prove how much he knows.

Emerging from behind a crowd of Jenn's cousins, I see my father slap my brother on the back, then put his arm around him. I think of the day years earlier when we drove down to the Dead Sea together—not the trip I already told you about, but a different one. Joseph, Ephraim, my dad, and I. Ephraim was twenty-one then; suffering from debilitating depression, he had recently dropped out of college. I remember sitting at a picnic table in front of the water; my father didn't like the way Ephraim was eating his sandwich, or maybe it was something else. He told Ephraim he was lazy, that he didn't understand the value of hard work. He told Ephraim it was no surprise he was a failure, that he would always be a failure, that everything he would ever do would amount to nothing.

As my brother stands to speak, his friends begin their heck-ling. I can feel the levels of male hormone in the room gathering steam, taking on the rhythmic motions of forward movement, pushing me farther to the periphery. It's almost time for the groom to begin the procession to meet his bride.

Mick, his guitar slung over his shoulder, the fiddler, and the banjo player assemble. They begin to play a melody, a melody without words, a melody weighted with sadness and solemnity that has accompanied Jewish couples to the wedding canopy for centuries. I rush back to my place among the women, where the bride is waiting for her groom—and then, suddenly, there he is, my little brother Ephraim, flanked on either side by Jenn's father and by our father, a sea of men swelled up behind them. The fid-dler fiddles, the banjo player strums. My brother approaches his bride and lifts the veil from her face. I can see that she has tears in her eyes, but they do not spill over.

The rituals of the Jewish wedding are not new to us. By the time I am sitting next to my sister at our middle brother's wed-ding, I have no remaining illusions about the safety or perma-nence of marriage, the emotional refuge offered by the wedding canopy. My parents' marriage has failed, my first marriage has failed, my sister's marriage has failed, Joseph's marriage is failing as we speak. But still, I cannot help it. I close my eyes and silently bless Ephraim that this time will be different. My sister is crying, and I am crying, and we keep wiping the corners of our eyes to keep the tears from ruining our makeup.

After the ceremony, there are pictures, and every permutation must be captured: the bride with the bride's parents; the groom with the groom's parents; the bride and groom with the bride's parents; the bride and groom with the groom's parents; the bride with her siblings; the groom with his siblings—all the variations in their infinite possibilities.

While the regular guests mingle in the main room, eating kosher pigs in blankets and mini quiches, we all stand around, awaiting instruction. The photographer bellows out the various combinations.

"Jenn's mom and dad!" he calls, and they take their place against the idyllic backdrop, Jenn's dad lovingly holding his wife's manicured hands.

"Ephraim's mom and dad!" the photographer calls out.

Dutifully, obediently, not wanting to cause a problem or disappoint my brother, my mother steps forward. So does my father. And as they do, the one thing I have been trying to prevent, slowly, finally, incomprehensibly, takes shape in front of my eyes. Against an unnaturally blue Lake Michigan, in front of all of his children, my father places his arm around my mother, enfolds her hand in his. And as he does, my mother's body shrinks, conserving all its resources, her eyes widening, her smile calcifying. I watch it like a nightmare unfolding in slow motion, the kind from which you wake up soaked in your own sweat.

I understand my father's logic; if there is a professional photograph of him and my mother at their son's wedding, a photo of them holding hands, he can continue to pretend that everything is as it had been—that he is still the rabbi, that my mother is still the rabbi's wife, that he still presides over his congregants, that he still has something to teach them.

"*No!*" I hear myself scream.

I'd assumed the photographer had been alerted beforehand, that all parties were informed.

But here again I am mistaken. Somehow it is still my job to protect my mother. Somehow it still falls to me to ensure the worst thing doesn't happen.

I turn to the photographer and address him directly. "Stop!" I yell. "Stop this right now!"

At this, my father promptly releases my mother's hand and curses under his breath. I know my father, know he wants to hurt me any way he can. Because there are people around, because a large crowd is, in fact, milling about just beyond the heavy glass doors at this very moment, he knows he cannot make it obvious. Instead, he walks right up to me and leans in close, the cedar and musk of his cologne mixing with his breath.

"Thanks a lot, Sara," he whispers, the faint spray of saliva hitting my face. Then he is gone, the heavy glass doors banging behind him.

"Well, I guess that's a wrap!" the photographer is saying. "Thank you all so much!" and everyone disperses.

My breath becomes shallow, my limbs tingly—I can feel what is happening inside me, the outer perimeter of panic, just as it is gathering momentum but before it reaches full speed. A problem now is that I am shaking. Another problem is that I feel like I can't breathe. My husband comes over and puts his arm around me.

"Why don't we get some fresh air?" he says.

"No," I say. I know he is trying to take care of me, but I don't want to let him.

"Come on, let's go for a walk," he says.

"No," I say, moving away from him, something loud and insistent thrumming in my brain. "I need to find my sister."

Inside the museum, the band begins to play. It is no secret that Jenn and her mother have planned the entire wedding; the only thing that matters to Ephraim is the music. He'd always said that if he ever got married, he wanted Buzzy Morris to play. Buzzy Morris, the master of the electric fiddle, the king of the blues violin, is a fixture at the bars Ephraim had been sneaking into since high school. Now Buzzy is here with his entire band—including a vocalist with a voice as deep as the Chicago River. Buzzy works his fiddle as they play the Jewish wedding song about how, on the outskirts of Jerusalem, the sounds of joy and gladness can still be heard, the voice of the groom, the voice of the bride. The Israeli cousins break into a hora, their hands clasped tightly together, the South Africans curling into a snake behind them. I can feel the sweat running in a rivulet down my back, the heat that is overtaking my whole body. I try to remember what my midwife told me about breathing, but my mind goes blank. I know now how wrong I was to think that I could ever take care of another person, how misguided I was to think that I was equipped to be a mother. I cut through the dancers, searching for my sister.

"I need a joint," I tell her.

I knew there was weed at the wedding. I had seen Nate and some of their high school friends sneaking puffs on the balcony. It was the only substance I'd discovered that could calm me when I felt like this.

"You're pregnant," my sister says.

"Thank you," I say. "I'm aware of that. Will you get it for me or not?"

"If you want, you should talk to Nate," she says, "but I can't be part of it."

I tell her to forget it. I tell her I am fine. The thing about my sister is she has patience for me until she doesn't. I walk quickly to the bathroom and lock myself in a stall. Through the doors, I can hear the band shifting gears, breaking into "Under My Thumb." I think that my baby can hear it too, because he starts to kick like crazy.

"What is it, baby?" I ask, and in response, he kicks some more. I place both hands on the globe of my belly and begin to sway. He's trying to tell me something, I can feel it. I look down at my feet. Somehow, after hours of elevation, I've managed to squeeze them into the peep-toe heels I'd naively purchased months earlier. By way of a miracle, they don't hurt.

I unlock the stall, wash my hands, blot my makeup with a paper towel, and make my way out to the dance floor. Joseph and Rachel are already dancing, my sister doing the low, swingy thing she does with her hips, Joseph moving as though without density. We are good children.

Because our parents love to dance, we love to dance; because they are light on their feet, we are light on our feet; because their hips are loose, our hips are loose. It was one of the things we all had in common. It was one of the things that made us a family.

I start to move, as though in a dream. Like everyone else, I'd grown up listening to a man sing this song, but now the woman with the voice like the Chicago River is singing it, and the words shift too. I dance, and I keep dancing, and I dance so hard that a couple of the South African cousins tap me on the shoulder and ask if I want to sit down and drink a glass of water, and I ignore them.

Suddenly, I am aware of my mother's friend Joanna, draped in a fur stole in August, trying to get my attention. She is gesticulating wildly, as though in emergency. She links her arms together like she's cradling an imaginary baby, trying to convey that I am somehow harming my unborn child, that if I keep dancing like this, I will surely give birth right here on the dance floor.

I do not give birth on the dance floor. My contractions begin three months later in our apartment in Jerusalem as a winter storm approaches. We take a taxi to the hospital, arriving just before snow blankets the city. I labor for hours, my fever spiking, an IV in my arm, my body convulsed with vomiting. I labor and labor with my husband and my mother and the midwife in the room, and I beg for them to help me, but they cannot help me. The baby is stuck. Or I am stuck. My body will not open itself enough to let the baby out.

"What is it?" the midwife asks, her hand on my forehead.

"My child!" I scream.

"What is it?" the midwife asks again, and I scream, "I don't want him to suffer!"

It isn't because I don't love my child that I don't want to bring him into this world. It's because I love my child that I don't want to bring him into this world. Because I know what I know about a parent's unhappiness, how it bleeds onto the child, how it bleeds no matter what.

Because I know what it feels like to feel your parent's sadness, to feel their sadness until it becomes your own, until you cannot tell where their sadness ends and where yours begins.

It's because I love my child that I don't want to bring him into this world. Because I know my child is happy now, happy where he is, that he is safe and protected, and I never want to take that away from him.

11

YOU ARE MY ANGEL

AT NIGHT, MY SON DOESN'T WANT TO SLEEP. Even after we've read three books, even after he's drunk his milk, even after we've watched our shadows on the wall. Even then, he doesn't want to sleep.

"I don't want to sleep," my son says.

He is two years old, and it is his right.

"You don't have to sleep," I tell him. "You can just rest."

We are lying together in the big bed, my arms wrapped around him, the room dark.

"Where's my shadow?" he asks.

"Your shadow's sleeping," I say.

He is quiet for a long moment. "My granola sleeping?"

"Yes, your granola's sleeping."

"My strawberries sleeping?" He says it like this: *stwaw-bawuhs.*

"Yes, your strawberries are sleeping."

Another long pause. He is thinking this over. "My car sleeping?"

"Yes."

"My fish sleeping?"

"Yes."

"My doggy sleeping?"

"Yes."

He's referring to his stuffed animals, which are usually dressed in his T-shirts.

"My trucks sleeping?"

"Umm . . . hmm . . ."

"Mommy, my trucks sleeping?"

"Yes, boo-boo, your trucks are sleeping."

This seems to satisfy him, because now he is on to the ABCs.

"A, B, C, D, E, F, G . . . where's Daddy?"

"Daddy's working."

"I want to work too."

"Not tonight, boo-boo. You can work tomorrow."

"I want to work right now!"

"It's not time for working. It's time for resting."

And then he's back to the ABCs, which he proceeds to sing three times in a row. Then "The Farmer in the Dell." *The farmer takes a wife, the farmer takes a wife.* What could it possibly mean to him for a farmer to take a wife? What is a farmer? What is a wife? In the dark, his small, sweet voice has the lilt of the divine.

Who is this creature that has burst into our lives? Where did he come from? Did he already bear the imprint of a thousand lifetimes, or is this his first time here? And how, of all the human beings on the planet, did we come to be his parents?

I put my face in his hair, his silky cornsilk hair, and whisper inside it, inside the dark, "You are my angel."

It is Friday night, but my husband is at work. It's a new job, a job we left Jerusalem for, a job he must prove himself at. I don't have a job, at least not a real one. When I wasn't taking care of my child, I was ghostwriting a sex guidebook for two doctors. It goes without saying that it wasn't really a book, just a guidebook. It goes without saying that I wasn't really a writer, just a ghost.

My husband was a writer, and he had achieved some of his dreams, coauthoring several books for well-regarded presses. But that did not pay us enough to live, and neither did my work. And so we had decided to move back to America, where my husband had accepted a job in the nonprofit sector, which provided health insurance and a retirement plan, even as I could see the dread in his eyes.

It's already been six months since we've been in this new place where I know nobody. Just my husband, who's at work all day, and my baby, who's mine to care for—and my mother, who's moved here with us too. We need help with the baby, and my mother offered the help; also, she has nowhere else to go. Ever since she left my father, she's had nowhere else to go.

Since my husband won't be home for dinner, I make vegetable lasagna and a salad with everything in it. For my son, I mash avocadoes and yams. My mother is here, but I am the one who cooks, the one who does the laundry, the one who wipes down the kitchen counters every night before I go to sleep. Every day it shocks me not to be a child anymore, that I am the one who acts, not the one who is acted upon.

Because it is Friday night, we light the candles—the only way that we still mark the Sabbath. We move our hands in front of our eyes and say the blessing together. My mother is no longer a religious woman, and I am no longer a religious woman. But when we light the candles, our bodies know what to do, our muscles remember before we do. My mother grabs a scarf from somewhere and ties it around her head.

There is no way for me to imagine being a mother without my mother. Even after everything, it was my mother who held my hand throughout my delivery, my mother who showed me how to rock my baby when he cried, my mother who bounced the baby on the ball for hours until he fell asleep.

As soon as my son could speak, he called her Ama, the soft consonant the universal sound of comfort.

I had never known my mother to drink, but ever since she left my father, she has started to drink a little on Friday nights. After half a glass of hard apple cider, she is already tipsy. She pours me a glass and one for herself, and we clink our glasses together while my son gnaws on a piece of bread in his high chair.

"*L'chaim*," I say.

"*L'chaim*," she says.

Sometimes, it's like the past thirty years have never happened, that my mother and I are meeting as friends, fellow travelers whose souls are inextricably intertwined. Other times, I ask her how she could have stayed with my father as long as she did, how she could have let those things happen to us.

"It's my brain!" she will say. "It's my brain! I couldn't understand who he was."

The thing that finally enabled my mother to leave my father after forty years was her realization that he was evil. Not that he did evil things or had acted in evil ways, but that he himself—the totality of his being—was evil. My mother needed an all-encompassing explanation for everything that had happened, and this was it. I didn't dismiss her theory as a possibility, but I also couldn't help noticing how convenient it was, how neatly it tied everything up, how much it absolved her of anything.

"Your father isn't human," she'd recently begun saying. "I know that's hard to hear."

Because the world had turned upside down and life had rearranged itself into a series of unrecognizable sequences, my mother had begun dating. This doesn't mean that she goes anywhere, only that she posted a picture of herself online and a trail of strange messages followed. We'll be sitting on the couch, the baby singing "Three Blind Mice," me reading a book, and all of a sudden, my mom will blurt out, "I've got a live one!"

But none of them ever amount to anything, and sometimes I wonder if they are even real. I pour myself another glass of cider and ask my mother if she's ever been in love.

"Once," she says.

"With who?"

I have no idea whom she might be referring to.

"With your father," she says, "with Danny."

It's an early spring day, cold and crisp and bracing. The sun is shining, and the water is rushing fast over the rocks in the creek bed, flush with melted snow, and it is this that my son notices first.

"Water!"

Now that he is two, every day brings a new approach to old words.

"Come on, let's keep walking to the bridge," I tell him.

"Bwidge!" he says and his face lights up. Almost anything can make him happy.

We are crouched down by the edge of the water, collecting rocks to throw into the creek—white river rocks, slate-colored rocks, pebbles as smooth as jelly beans—when my uncle calls. My father's younger brother.

"I need to talk to you," he says. "It's serious."

He doesn't ask me if it's a good time or tell me to sit down or inquire if I'm with my child. He is the head of a large company, after all; I am just a mother. Between the two of us, there is no question as to whose time is more valuable.

He tells me my father is dying. That it's an advanced form of cancer, that by the time the doctors found it, it had already reached his bladder. He has six months left to live, two years if he's lucky, as though we were still operating in the realm of luck.

"It's serious," he says. "Your dad wants to talk to you."

By now, it has been nearly three years since I've seen my father. I have never informed him of my son's birth, did not invite him to the bris, never even sent a photo. I have already spent so much of my life living in my father's shadow, inhabiting the same shadows he inhabits. I finally decided I could not do it anymore. I want my son's life to mark a new beginning, a new history that did not include the immediate past.

"If you have any thought of seeing him," my uncle is saying, "any thought at all of seeing your father before he goes, now is the time."

My vision blurs in front of me. Or maybe my vision is fine, and it's the world itself that's moving at a different speed.

"Mommy, look!" my son says. "A duck!"

"We have to go home," I tell him. "We have to go home right now."

"Why, Mommy?" my son says, but I don't answer because I cannot think.

I am packing up his diaper bag, with his diapers and his bottle and his bag of peeled apple slices, and I am shaking. My whole body is shaking.

"Let's go," I tell him. "It's time to go."

I have never said a word about my father to my son, never once mentioned his existence. How can I explain to him that his grandfather is about to die, his grandfather he doesn't know is living?

I strap my son into his stroller and begin the climb uphill, up the path that will lead us to our house.

The last time I saw my father was at my brother's wedding in Chicago, but that isn't what I am thinking about. I am thinking about the second-to-last time I'd seen him, in Jerusalem, when I was pregnant.

It was a Sabbath afternoon in the summer, the kind of afternoon when the sun beat down on everything. I should have been at home resting, but instead my husband and I took a taxi to the fanciest hotel in the city, where my father was staying as a guest. He could never afford a hotel like that on his own; he'd been flown in to perform the bar mitzvah of the son of former congregants who had since moved to Dallas.

"I'm getting the full VIP treatment," he told us when we met him in the lobby. He gave me a dry kiss and nodded at my belly before leaning into my ear and whispering, "Bet you didn't know your father was a VIP."

Bet you're right, I thought. By then, he'd already lost his second pulpit as well as his wife and any status he may have once had. He had only this—the occasional bar mitzvah or wedding gig—the kind of life cycle events at which he'd always excelled. Before we left, he embraced me and said, "If I die before the baby is born, I hope you'll name him after me."

There was never any way to escape it, the sadness I felt for my father.

Now there was more sadness coming, a sadness that was about to split and multiply, reproduce itself in an infinite number of iterations. I had no idea what would make me less sad, to see my father before he died or to never see him again.

When we get home, my mother is there waiting for us, holding open the screen door as though she can feel it, as though she knows what's coming.

My mother sees my face, and right away she knows, maybe not the details, but she knows.

"What happened?" she says. "Tell me what happened."

"He's dying," I tell her, and I don't have to say who. "He's dying," I say, and right away her body gives way. She collapses right there in my living room, because her body is no longer a structure that can support its own weight.

"I killed him," she sobs. "I killed him."

I could see that my mother was no longer an adult. In that moment, she was no longer a mother, but a daughter. A daughter who had always blamed herself for the fact that her mother had died. A daughter who still blamed herself for everything. Maybe if she'd been better, she'd always believed, nothing bad would have happened.

"You didn't kill him," I tell her. "You didn't kill him."

And I wonder again why it's my job, even now, to reassure her.

I am giving my son a bath, and the water is running, and his dolphin and dinosaurs are in the water too.

"Time to wash your face," I say, but he bats away the washcloth with his hand. Instead, he has a question.

"Mommy, do you have a mommy and also you are a mommy?"

"That's exactly right. Do you know who my mommy is?"

"Who?"

"Ama!"

He takes this in.

"And do you know that Daddy has a daddy and is also a daddy? Do you know who Daddy's daddy is?"

"Who?"

"Nini!"

"And who is Daddy's mommy?"

"Mimi!"

"And do we sometimes go to visit them?"

"Yes, we do."

He looks at me for a minute, and I can see the wheels turning in his brain. "Who is your daddy?"

There's no reason this question should surprise me, and yet it does. I have never said a word to him about his phantom grandfather, this man who doesn't exist. Maybe I never said anything because then I could pretend everything was fine. But my son was with me at the creek that day and has been with me every day since. Maybe he can sense that something's coming even if he cannot name it. He's a baby, but he isn't stupid.

I don't know what to say, and so I say the quickest, simplest thing that I can think of.

"I don't have a daddy," I tell him.

He looks up at me with his big blue eyes. I don't like lying to him, but there is also no way for me to tell him the truth: That I have a daddy, but he is sick. That I have a daddy, but I cannot be around him. That I have a daddy who's about to die.

What if I told you that I missed my dad. Would that make me crazy? If you are reading this, you know my father has done terrible things, but there are other things you should know too. Like the week before my second wedding, when I was flat broke and I called my dad and asked if he could bring me $300 so I could get my hair done the day-of. I knew I could ask him because I knew he wouldn't hesitate, because I knew he would want me to be happy on my wedding day, to have everything my heart desires.

Jewish tradition holds that parents do not choose their children—it's the children who choose their parents. How do they choose? From heaven, they approach every person who could potentially be their parent and select the ones who will love them the most. How does a soul, a baby not yet born, know who will love her the most? Because she can see in her mother's and father's eyes how much they've been longing for her.

This idea cannot be found in the tractates of the Talmud nor in the Five Books of Moses. It's the teaching of an obscure Hassidic rebbe, a teaching handed down, like so much of the Torah, from rabbi to student in the form of a story.

In this regard, I wasn't angry at my father, I was angry at myself. What kind of broken soul would choose him for a parent? In this case, the failing was mine.

The water is still running when my son asks, "Why you don't have a daddy?"

"That's just how it is for some people," I say. "Not everyone gets to have a mommy and daddy—"

I can feel myself veering off course, wading into murky waters. I don't want him to have to think about this, to imagine that a life without parents is possible. I want this to be a happy story; I am terrified of traumatizing him, and I try to bring it back around, to end on an upbeat note. "That's why you're so lucky to have a mommy and daddy who love you so much," I say.

I had made myself a promise that, when I had a child, I would always tell him the truth. But how can I tell him the truth? How can I look at his sweet face and tell him that there are parents who hurt their children, who hurt them over and over, that there are parents who hurt their children in so many different ways?

As soon as I wake up, I can feel the weight of the day pushing up against me, trying to crush me. It's a Sunday, and every act feels impossible. Getting out of bed, making a cup of coffee, fixing a bowl of oatmeal for my son. Soon we have to leave because we're already late for brunch at my in-laws, who live twenty-five minutes away in their big house surrounded by stuff.

"Do I have to go?" I say to my husband.

"Are you really going to do this again?" he says.

Since we moved, our marriage has changed. My husband was stressed because of his new job; he didn't like it, and if he didn't like it, what was he supposed to do? We had moved here for this job, and he had a family to support, and after paying rent, there was already so little left over. I could see his unhappiness, could feel it building. But how could I help him? I was drowning, drowning under a gigantic wave.

At my in-laws' house, there are so many things. A pantry full of family-sized boxes of brownie mix, piles of clothes bought on sale, flat-screen televisions in every room, even the bathrooms, the patio furniture out on the patio and the patio furniture covers necessary to protect the patio furniture—all the spoils of plenty, the loot from a lifetime of work.

"Look at this, Sara!" my mother-in-law says as she thrusts a bejeweled finger in my face with all the excitement of a young bride. "Walter bought it for me for our anniversary! After fifty years, I told him it was time for a *real* diamond!"

"Wow," I say, "that's amazing."

Over brunch, my mother-in-law regales us with news of her next diet, while her husband, a semi-retired scientist, looks down at the table before silently rising and clearing the plates.

On the way home, the highway is gray and endless, and the cars are gray and endless too. I think about the other people in their cars, people who have convinced themselves there is somewhere they have to go or someplace they have to be—maybe some of them, like me, on their way home from somewhere they never wanted to go in the first place.

All the people in their cars on the highway. What was it for? That was the question no one wants you to ask—not as a child and definitely not as an adult, since by then you're already supposed to know.

We exit the highway and pass the strip malls selling calling cards and discount furniture. It's almost dark, and it's started to rain. We're stopped at a red light when I see a mother pushing her child in a stroller, running to take shelter under a bus stop as night falls. The world has always felt to me like a collection of a million different sadnesses. Sometimes I could feel them all crashing down on me, crushing me at once.

The weight of the leaden sky crushes me.

The feeling of our car hitting a pothole crushes me.

The awareness that I feel this way while my son is sitting in the back seat looking peacefully out the window crushes me.

"What's wrong?" my husband says.

"Nothing," I tell him because there is nowhere to begin.

I curl into a fetal position in my seat and start to cry.

My husband grips the steering wheel and stares icily ahead. He is tired of all of it. "I can't believe you're going to ruin another Sunday," he says.

How can I tell him that I cannot ruin a day that is already ruined? *You cannot blame me for making a sad day sadder,* I want to say, but I know he won't know what I mean, so instead I say, "Where is your love for me when I need it the most?"

I look in the back seat at my son sitting in his car seat looking out the window, and think of what my mom said the last time we took him to the creek.

"He's so sweet," my mom said. "I never want anything bad to happen to him."

"I know," I told her. "Neither do I."

Of course I agreed with my mom, anyone would. But instead of filling me up, her words hollowed me out. Wasn't I once so sweet? Why didn't she never want anything bad to happen to me? I could feel this knowledge sitting somewhere inside me—the knowledge that some children are deemed worthy of protection and others are not.

The tears start to roll out now, long and slow and sonorous. All my life, I promised myself I'd be nothing like my parents. That if I ever had kids, I would give them a good life. I would make them feel safe. But now here I was, showing my child that nothing was safe, that the ground could shift, fissure, buckle beneath him at any moment and send us into free fall.

"What's wrong, Mommy?" he says.

"Mommy's not feeling well," I say.

I look at my husband, his face hardened.

"I help you, Mommy," my son says.

Inside my head, the words appear like an emergency flashing sign on a highway—

YOU ARE FAILING YOURSELF
YOU ARE FAILING YOUR CHILD

What kind of mother was I? Not the kind I'd imagined, not the kind I could be proud of, not the kind who could protect her child, not even from herself.

The wave passes, and there I am, left sitting in a film of my own terror in the front seat of the car.

I know things cannot go on as they are. I would have to do better, and in order to do better, I would have to remember one thing. That I was the adult, not the child, that I was no longer a daughter, but a mother.

At night, my son doesn't want to sleep. Even after we've read three books, even after he's drunk his milk, even after we've watched our shadows on the wall. Even then, he doesn't want to sleep.

"Where's my shadow?" he asks.

We are lying in bed, and I have just turned off the light.

"Your shadow went to sleep," I tell him, like I tell him every night.

"My shadow no go to sleep!" he says.

"Your shadow didn't go to sleep?" I ask.

"No! My shadow went away," he says.

"You're right, my love, your shadow went away. Your shadow goes away when it's dark."

My son strokes my cheek. The lights are out, but I can see his eyes shining in the darkness. He puts his hand against my face and says, "You're so nice, Mommy. You're my angel."

12

WELCOME TO MIAMI

IN THE END, WE DO GO TO MIAMI. But it is not to see my father. It is my brother we go to see, my baby brother, who was no longer a baby but, somehow, a man. To me, he would always be a baby. A baby lost at sea. A baby in a basket. A baby without its mother.

"I'm going to Miami," my sister told me one night on the phone. "I need to spend time with Noam. I need to talk to him in person."

"If you're going, we're going too," I said.

I couldn't keep watching while this thing called my brother's life unfolded. Every day, I tried to prepare myself for the worst thing that could happen, which wasn't even death. By any definition, he needed help. After things had fallen apart for him in LA, he came to the place that was the lowest place he could imagine, a place where he guessed he was least likely to be judged. When my brother fell out for the last time with his band, he lost his place to live. He had been staying with a series of friends, but now he wasn't welcome there either. And so he went down to Miami Beach and moved in with my dad.

"He is hated, and I am hated. I have that in common with him" is how he put it to me after the fact.

But that was not the only thing they had in common. My brother had a drug problem. And, as I was slowly piecing together, so did my father.

"So are you really living with Dad?" I'd ask on the phone.

"Nah, I just stay by him sometimes," he'd say. My brother half-pretended, half-lied, half-avoided, and after a while, I stopped asking.

Still, we knew the truth: he was thirty years old and couldn't afford a place of his own or even a place with roommates because he couldn't hold down a job. Since high school, he'd sold kitchen knives, vacuum cleaners, discounted pet supplies. He'd worked in an after-school program for little kids, and at a doggy day care. He'd painted houses and worked construction. He'd been a waiter, a driver for a car service, and probably some other things I would never know about.

Allegedly, he was working on his music. He told us he'd found a producer in Miami who was interested in recording some of his songs. Soon, he'd have an album, he told us. We were smart enough to know that, even if those things were true, they were only partial truths, thin slivers of the whole story. Over the years, my siblings and I had offered our homes, our couches, our guest bedrooms. We'd offered plane tickets and train tickets. We'd written him long letters. We'd looked him in the eye and talked to him straight. He would nod and say he agreed, and tell us he heard us, and then everything would just keep being the way it was.

In this regard, my imagination was an active, potent force. My brother could kill my father, or my father could kill my brother. They could each die of an overdose, together or alone. I pictured police cars, an ambulance, the door broken down, neighbors gathered, the diligence of the emergency medical technicians, the sound of the siren filling the humid night air. We had to go down and get our brother out.

We were going to see my brother, but the truth was we were going to see my father too. It was hard to admit, even to myself, that I wanted to see him before he died. I had no illusions that there would be any kind of grand farewell or that we might reach some tearful understanding. I just wanted to see him again.

"I'm not sure this is the best idea," my mother said when I informed her of the trip. "Is this really what you need right now?"

My mother was still living with us then; her opinion could not be avoided.

"I'm concerned, to be honest," my husband told me late one night after the baby was asleep. "We can't afford for you to lose three weeks where you can't get out of bed."

I was concerned too. I feared my own fragility, my tendency to fissure, crack, clatter to the floor. But it wasn't only myself I feared. I also feared my father, because I knew what he was capable of. There was always the chance he could do the worst thing possible. This wasn't my imagination. It was what he did the last time one of us went down to see him.

It was the previous spring, when my sister decided to bring her thirteen-year-old daughter to visit her grandfather one last time. My niece was the first of my parents' grandchildren, and even my father seemed to adore her, in his way. My sister's no dummy, nor is she prone to an excess of sentimentality. "I'm not expecting anything," she told me before she left for the airport.

It was less than twenty-four hours into her visit when she texted to let us know that our father had landed himself in the hospital. He had fallen off a chair and cut his face. It was Noam who found him. Noam who called 911. My sister rushed to the hospital. They didn't know if the fall was related to his cancer or to a recent change in medication. The nurses in the ER scurried around him, ordering tests and peppering him with questions.

"What's the most important thing we need to know about you?" a nurse asked.

"I'm clergy," he said—his two favorite words, the two words that solved everything. As she left the room, my father called out to her, "God bless you."

It was only once the nurses had disappeared that my father told my sister the truth: He had overdosed on crack. He was a sixty-eight-year-old man wearing reading glasses and orthopedic shoes, and he had overdosed on crack.

"I made a big mistake," he told her. "I took a hit of crack and fell over." He implored her not to tell the doctors or anyone in our family.

The fact was my father could have picked any time of the year to overdose. Did he have to do it on the single day that his daughter and granddaughter were making the trip down to see him? Did he want to be cruel, and if so, why? That was the question I could never answer. Was it out of habit or just for sport? He always had to do something to draw all the attention back to him, where he needed it. I tried to picture what he must look like hunched over a crack pipe, wanting to smoke enough so that he alights on a high from which he will never return. He wanted to die. Everyone knew that. But now I had the facts in front of me of how he would do it.

After that, my sister swore she would never see him again, that she would never so much as step foot in the state of Florida as long as she lived. But our father had our kryptonite, a secret weapon. He had our brother. We didn't know if he was plying him with drugs or money or if our brother felt so shitty about himself, he didn't think he deserved anything else but to be sharing a filthy, one-room studio with a person who liked to throw phones at his head.

As usual, Noam was not responding to my emails or calls. The last text I sent him read: *Hi #5, We are coming this week-end to Miami, Friday afternoon to Monday afternoon. Can't wait to hang out. Love, #1.*

I employed the parlance he had invented, in which we referred to each other by our place in the birth order. "My bookends," my mother called us. I tried to keep the tone light and lively, as though we just happened to be coming to town. I didn't want to scare him off, since he was prone to being scared off.

The night before our flight—after dinner, after putting the baby to bed—I can feel it coming. The waves of nausea, coming on slow, then fast, cresting and crashing as I lean over the toilet bowl, the white porcelain cool against my cheek. The vomiting comes over and over again, knocking me out, chaining me to an undertow.

I think of all the stories my father had told me about growing up in Miami Beach—the dock behind their family home, jumping into Biscayne Bay with his sisters and brother, their house with the circular driveway filled with the Civil War–era portraits his father collected, flush with new money from the American dream. My father talked about Miami so often and with such fervor that when I was little I thought he was saying *my ami*, as though everyone in the world had an *ami*, that one special place that lived forever in their memory.

Even as a child, I knew the story my father was telling wasn't the whole story, that even if my father's words were true, there were other truths. Like those I'd heard in pieces from my father's older sister Auntie Sonia—Danny protecting their mother when their father went after her, Danny the object of their father's never-ending fury, Danny standing guard at the top of the driveway with a baseball bat, the asphalt hot in the summer night, watching, waiting, making sure his father didn't return.

It didn't matter that my own life was deteriorating—that my husband and I were fighting all the time, that I had not made a single friend in this new place where we lived, that I couldn't manage to finish the novel I'd been working on for years, even though every year I promised myself I would. My obligation now was to go to Miami Beach, to solve something that had started years before I was born, to solve something that had started even before my father was born, to solve something that, in all probability, could never be solved.

We touch down in Miami, get our bags from baggage claim, find the shuttle to the rental-car place, fill out the paperwork, locate the compact, two-door sedan in the lot, and hit the causeway. As we drive, the art deco hotels rise up around us, built by mob money around the same time my father's parents moved here from the tenements of Williamsburg, Brooklyn, and Paterson, New Jersey, respectively—my grandfather promising my grandmother a house on the water, a house full of children, an automobile. He had started his own business importing produce from Panama. He liked to dream big.

I didn't know where we were staying, only that my husband had booked it last minute; I hoped it was, at least, clean. Going down to Miami for the weekend was not something we had ever done before. We weren't those kinds of people; if it weren't for me, my husband likely would have forgotten his swimsuit.

It is September, but it feels like the dead of summer. We blast the air-conditioning until goose bumps erupt on our skin and the sweat under our armpits turns cold. We drive by the squat pastel estates hugging the bay, then turn a corner, and my stomach lurches.

There, columned and domed, a landmark of Byzantine architecture taking up several city blocks, its stained glass windows refracting the light from a tropical sun, is one of the oldest, wealthiest, and most stately synagogues in America. Inscribed on its imposing façade, surrounded by teetering palm trees, is its name, which in Hebrew means "God is with us."

It is the synagogue of my father's youth, the synagogue where he'd celebrated his bar mitzvah, the synagogue to which he'd returned five decades later, like a prodigal son, to be its spiritual leader. It was a plum position, a temple right by the beach with a well-endowed membership, the answer, we thought, to my father's unhappiness. His homecoming after so many cold seasons in Chicago. But like so many things, we'd been mistaken.

We turn onto Collins Avenue, and suddenly we are pulling into a semicircular driveway, and a smiling man in crisp white shorts is opening my car door and talking to me like he knows me, like he has been waiting all day for my arrival.

Like any married person, I sometimes feel disappointed in my husband. If I am not careful, I can let my disappointment color everything. He could take better care of himself, speak more calmly to our son when he's stressed, stop leaving half-filled coffee cups all over the house. On a bad day, I blame my husband for the thousands of ways I feel let down in my life. Then, every once in a while, he does something that so overwhelms and surprises me that I remember that he is not all bad, that he is, in fact, not that far from being the man I once dreamed of.

We revolve into the doorway and get in line at reception, and I have, briefly, the sensation of stepping into someone else's life. The lobby is filled with low-slung, armless couches upholstered in cool, understated fabrics. Some curve, like snakes, around glass-topped tables. In the center of the room, a dimly lit chandelier, made of hundreds of glass balls, hangs suspended over the bar like a glowing spaceship. Through the windows, I can see the yellow-and-white-striped cabanas surrounding the pool.

Our bags are whisked away, and soon we find ourselves in a room with a balcony overlooking the ocean and high-lofted beds with crisp, white sheets, an armchair covered in a large palm print. I walk into the bathroom, which references the mid-century but is all gorgeously new. It is not literal Miami style, but a wink at Miami style. Everything is beautiful, and everyone is so nice.

We close the door.

"I cannot believe you did this. How did you do this?" I ask my husband as I walk around turning the light switches on and off. "No, seriously, how did you do this?"

He explains to me the beauty of the Internet and tells me a tale of a magical place where last-minute hotel deals could be had for a fraction of the price.

"Call my sister," I tell him, since I know she had landed the night before.

Within fifteen minutes, she is at our door, and within another five, we are lying together in the big bed, propped up against our hotel pillows, eating the organic, chocolate-covered pretzels that came gratis with the room, and flipping through the channels, Rachel stopping on the sports channels, while I advocate for *House Hunters International*. My husband is already out on the porch, talking on the phone. I can hear his bursts of laughter through the sliding-glass door.

"Can you believe we're here?" I ask my sister.

"No. Can you?"

"No."

"Dad keeps calling me. He wants to see us. He wants to take us out to dinner. Let's just get it over with."

"Okay, let's do it tomorrow night."

"Fine. I'll text him."

"Dad knows how to text?"

"I don't know, but I don't want to talk to him on the phone."

"Kill me."

"Kill me first."

"No, *you* kill *me* first. I called it."

"Okay, Big Sis, whatever you say." She says this in her baby-girl voice, the one she uses when she plays the role of the obedient and adoring little sister, which is the joke.

There is a knock at the door, which always makes us jumpy.

"Who is that?" I ask her in a panic.

"Relax, it's just Noam." She goes to open the door.

There he is, suddenly: a person in the flesh, not a story in my mind that I am always writing and rewriting. He looks good; his face and body a little more filled out than when I'd seen him six months ago, his skin clear, his hair neatly cropped. He's wearing black Levi's and a white T-shirt, a variation on his uniform. It is a relief to see him in person. He is here. He is okay.

"Noam!" I throw my arms around him, and then I know he is not okay.

He stinks. His T-shirt stinks, his pants stink, and up close to his body, I can smell the odor drifting up from his black gym shoes. Everything stinks, like sweat and stale smoke and weed and unhappiness. Did my sister notice it too? Neither of us said a word. The whole point was to keep things cool.

We watch an episode of *Project Runway*, a bit of the Kardashians. We finish the pretzels and then the root-vegetable chips. We are hungry. My husband wants Cuban food.

"Do you know a good place?" he asks Noam.

"Oh yeah, this place where my friend Ibrahim used to work. It's chill."

"Do we have to drive?" Jeremy asks. "Parking's gonna be a pain in the ass."

"Nah, we can walk."

"How long is it?" I ask. "I'm starving."

"Yeah, it's just up Collins."

As soon as we step outside, I curse myself for my lack of preparedness. The heat, even in the dark, surpasses my expectations. My jeans and cotton blouse stick to my skin. My entire face, not just my forehead and upper lip, is soon slick with sweat. We move through the night in pairs—Jeremy and Rachel up ahead, Noam and I trailing behind them. In the dark, the strip seems endless, hotel after hotel after hotel, all filled with people pouring into cars or disappearing behind revolving glass doors.

People don't come to South Beach to be sad. They come to have fun. To stay in a hotel with valet parking and put on their Louboutins and hit the W Hotel. They get tanned, waxed, and blown out. They go out on the town, marching down Collins Avenue in groups and pairs like soldiers in an army whose mission—whose sole purpose—is to have fun.

My brother seems to know each of these hotels, not for the times he stayed in them or ordered drinks in their lobbies,

but for his friends who had worked in them as busboys, bell-
boys, bartenders.

"See that?" he asks me, pointing to the tower rising on our
left, its balconied floors awash in a sherbet-colored glow. "My
friend Louis used to work there." A few steps later, he points to
an even grander hotel, the Grand Tropic.

"I once applied for a job there, but I didn't get it."

For a minute, I want to ask him what the job was, why he
thinks he wasn't hired, what kind of job he might look for next.
Instead, I say, "How much longer?"

"Yeah, it's just up here," he says, pointing vaguely in the distance.

With every step, my body grows heavier. I'd only slept a few
hours the previous night, and I can feel the brininess in my stomach.
We've been walking for thirty minutes. I am not drinking enough
water. Up ahead, I can see my husband and sister waiting for us
at the crosswalk, the back of my husband's shirt soaked through.

"So where's the place, brother?" my husband asks when we
catch up.

"Yeah, I'm not really sure. Maybe up by Washington."

"Do you know the name of it? I can look it up on my phone,"
my husband says, but Noam can't remember.

It is a Friday night. Shabbat. The holiest night of the year,
even if it comes every week. That is the paradox of holiness. It
doesn't have to be rare; it is there waiting for you all the time.
It is Shabbat, but we are not sitting down together as a family. My
mother did not bake challah, or roast a chicken, or make soup.
She is sleeping at her boyfriend's house in Virginia, where she
spends every weekend now. My son is at my sister-in-law's house,
probably eating macaroni and cheese in front of a television show;
my dad is in his one-room apartment, reliably high and alone.

My other brothers are scattered, in Chicago and Canada, and here were the rest of us, the survivors of our family's dissolution, wandering the avenue of a city our grandparents had settled in seventy years earlier, filling their big house by the bay with children and oil paintings, with new cars and books and pony rides. That is all gone now, and I am tired.

"I think I'm gonna go," I tell them.

"Go where?" my sister asks.

My brother looks off into the distance.

"Back to the hotel. I just need to lie down."

I look at my sister's and brother's faces, blank-faced and bathed in film against the lit-up night. They are used to me leaving abruptly. They know there is nothing they can say.

"I'll get you a cab," my husband says.

"Where to, miss?" the cab driver asks, and it fills me with relief that he calls me miss and that I can give him the name of a hotel where I can get into bed and disappear.

In the elevator on the way up, I am accompanied by two young women, their faces and bodies aglow with bronzer.

"It's *my* bachelorette party," one says to the other. "If she wants to be left out, that's up to her."

"I *told* you, Suki," the other girl says.

When I insert the credit-card key into the door and the green light beeps, I take a breath. Here is a room where I can be alone, where I can climb into bed and close my eyes, the closest thing to the Sabbath I could imagine.

The next morning, we pick up Noam and Rachel to get breakfast. We decide on the Pink Palace, which is entirely pink. We sit in the heat, Noam fanning my sister with a menu, until our table's ready. She is nauseated. We are taking turns being sick; how can we not? There are no rituals to guide us through what we are about to undertake, no protocols, no words of comfort to fall back on. There is just the hard, blunt fact of preparing to face our father.

After breakfast, my sister and I go to the beach, just the two us. It is a perfect day, the sky blue, with only a faint sketching of white clouds on the horizon. We see the water from the board-walk and walk toward it. Somehow, it isn't crowded, only a few umbrellas doting the sand. The fishy smell of seaweed fills our nostrils, and we breathe it in. A little yellow airplane flies over-head pulling a sign that reads: SINFUL SATURDAYS AT THE KING OF DIAMONDS! TONIGHT!!!

"What are we doing here?" I ask her.

She gives her world-weary laugh.

"Truth and reconciliation?"

We are both quiet for a while. Then she says: "To be present."

We are feeling thoughtful. Also, a little stoned. We'd shared a joint at her place before setting out. That night, we'd be seeing our father. The last time I'd seen him was at Ephraim's wedding in Chicago three years earlier, right before I gave birth. I look out at the blue-green ocean and think about how much has changed since then, and how much change is coming.

That night, we drive to my father's apartment building to pick him up for dinner. The first thing I think when I see him is how diminished he looks. Diminished in size, diminished in stature, diminished by illness. His hair has gone white. His clothes hang on his thin frame. He has let his stubble grow out. Peeking out of the waistband of his relaxed-fit khakis is a small plastic yellow top connected to the clear plastic bag that collects his bodily waste. He has shape-shifted again. He is diminished in every way.

My father's building faces a few palm trees and a massive parking lot. We stand at the edge of the lobby, which boasts not a single adornment, as we wait for him to descend. When he appears, it is on the arm of my brother, as though he is a groom being led to the bridal canopy. In South Beach, my parents had lived in a gated building with a crystal chandelier and a view of the water, but North Miami is not South Miami. We can't see the ocean from here, only parked cars.

Because he is my father, he does not come empty-handed. In this case, he has brought an oversized cardboard envelope filled with papers. Due to muscle weakness or the need for a semi-dramatic gesture, he is unable to carry it, and so on this occasion, his gift is carried in the arms of my brother. We say hello and exchange brief hugs, and then my father is eager to show what he's brought for me.

"Noam!" he stage-yells left, grabbing hold of my brother's arm. "Give her the package!"

As we stand on the strip of concrete separating the parking lot from the lobby, as the stadium parking lot lights bear down on us, my brother hands me the envelope.

"Sara, this is for you," my father says.

"What's in it?"

"I have no idea. This and that. You'll have to look through it." He makes a gesture to indicate that he is too busy to spend his time going through old papers, which is the furthest thing from the truth. He knows exactly what is in the envelope; he just doesn't want to tell me.

"Thank you," I say. "I want to wait until we're sitting down so I can open it."

I pretend I want to give the contents of the envelope their due, but the truth is I can't imagine what might be inside, and part of me doesn't want to know. He nods solemnly.

"Smart idea," he says.

He was always good at praising me for the small things.

On the way over, we'd done a quick search and come up with a small Italian restaurant with good online reviews. When we arrive, we discover that it too faces a parking lot. It is a Saturday night, a night when my father, under normal circumstances, would be returning home from synagogue and we'd make havdalah, gathered around the braided candlestick in our darkened living room as my father chanted the prayer and we made our way through the rituals we knew so well: examining our fingernails by the light of the flame; taking turns smelling cinnamon from the spice box to guide us into a sweet new week; drowning the flame in a puddle of wine. When I was very young, we would hold hands and dance in a circle, singing, "Elijah the Prophet, Elijah the exalted."

Tonight, there will be no havdalah—no ceremony to separate the sacred from the ordinary, no words of comfort to accompany us in the Sabbath's wake. There is just us: my father, my sister, my brother, my husband and me, sitting on the patio facing a wall of cars, ordering calorie-dense food in the stifling heat. An industrial-sized fan oscillates from side to side as we decide on the garlic bread, the pizza, the caprese salad, the pasta alfredo. My father orders the chicken marsala. There is no thought to keeping kosher. We were just another godless family eating at a mid-range restaurant on a Saturday night in North Miami.

"How's Joe?" my father asks, using not just my son's name, but his nickname, as though he'd seen him last week, as though he'd been bouncing him on his knee and taking him to the park all along.

For the first time since he'd been born, the sound of my son's name makes me uneasy. I had never called my father to tell him of the birth, never sent a photo, never even told him his name. And yet somehow he knew it, which meant he had talked about my son with someone, an uncle or cousin, perhaps, that he had a picture of him in his mind.

"He's great." I don't want to say any more, don't want to belabor the obvious: that my father is a phantom grandfather, a man my son has never, and will never, meet. A ghost in pictures who one day I will tell my son is dead.

All through dinner, I sit in near silence, half-eating my food, half-listening as my father regales Jeremy with complaints about his stoma bag: it was cheaply made, it leaked, it was difficult to put in. "You can't imagine," he says to Jeremy. "And I hope you never have to."

From time to time, Jeremy makes empathetic noises. "Wow, Danny," I hear him say at one point. "That sounds really rough."

Our server, a youngish woman with an Italian accent, is remarkably attentive, refilling our water glasses at every opportunity and removing each dish as it is finished, then plying us with coffee and dessert.

"How's the espresso?" my father asks.

"Excellent, sir. Our coffee we bring from Italy."

He turns to us. "Anyone want an espresso?"

For us, it is too late and too hot for caffeine. We shake our heads.

"*Un caffè*," he smiles at her, employing his fake Italian accent, raising an index finger.

The waitress smiles back, and for a moment, I can see how she might see him, a charming older gentleman, out for a family meal with his children. This quality of his—his need to ingratiate himself to strangers, to impress anyone he encounters, to play the role of indulgent paterfamilias, was something that, back when he was my father, filled my blood vessels with rage and my organs with shame. My rage is gone now, and all I can see are the sad ministrations of a man who can't stop trying to feel important.

Things are moving to a close. The night is wrapping up. If I am going to open the envelope in my father's presence, which I know is what he wants, this is the time.

And so I remove it from the seat next to me, unwinding the string closure in a counterclockwise motion, opening the cardboard flaps carefully, as though it were a real gift.

It is not this and that. It is all the birthday and Mother's Day cards my mother had ever received, dating back to 1981, when it was just me and my sister, and I was the only one who was functionally literate. Hundreds of cards in all, spanning thirty years, pristinely preserved and meticulously organized in chronological order, from all of her five children.

It is not a gift for me at all. It is a message I am meant to deliver to my mother.

He's thinking of you, Mom. He loves you. This man you married, this man with whom you brought five children into the world, he's a good man. See, look at the evidence, the fruits of your labor. He didn't throw any of it away.

I don't know what to say, so I say the first thing that pops into my head, which is, "Mom is going to be really happy to have these," and then immediately regret it, knowing the mere mention of her could set him off.

But he plays it cool. "Well, I don't know how much longer I'll be around, and I thought you should have them."

Anything recognizable about our family had slid into the past, slowly and then all at once. My dad had not been a good father, but he never left us. All those days packed into weeks, then years, then decades, all those days he made his way home from synagogue by himself. The bills he paid. The groceries he brought home. Now there was a whole family that no longer wanted anything to do with him. I could see the picture of him, aged four or five, in his white cap and gown, upon graduating from nursery school, with his blond hair and blue eyes and ready smile. I could always see that boy in my head.

Suddenly, I couldn't remember why I wasn't in touch with him. He was still my father. He had given me life. He had given me money. He had helped me with my homework. What about the time in high school when I was representing Canada at the model UN and he stayed up all night writing my position paper, so that when I woke up in the morning, it was all there, in his downward-slanting all-caps script, torn from his yellow legal pad, tucked into a blue folder? Or the time after a snowstorm when he drove me and my sister up to Wisconsin for the day to go skiing, while my mom stayed home with the little kids, and he let me listen to my new Madonna tape the whole way?

Now he is sick and alone, and I don't know why I've left him for dead.

We drive him back to his apartment, mostly in silence, with him making small talk along the way about the palm trees, the weather, the light traffic, the light rain that was beginning to fall.

I say nothing, just look out the window into the dark, lonely cars racing down the causeway. When we reach my father's apartment complex, a part of me hopes he'll invite us up, to see the home he has made for himself, to see how our father lives now. But he doesn't, and a part of me is grateful that he knows enough to spare us that.

The next morning, we have the talk we'd come here to have.

My sister and I are sitting on the big bed, the TV humming in the background, Noam in one chair, Jeremy in another. With what I hope is an imperceptible eye movement, I signal to Jeremy and Rachel that we can't wait anymore.

"So, can we talk for a minute?" Jeremy says. He has a way of being nonthreatening.

"Yeah, sure," my brother says, like he'd been waiting for this moment all along.

"We just want to reflect back what you've told us," Jeremy says. "It seems like you're not in the best place. Living in Miami, living with D.N.S., it seems like those things aren't making you happy."

That was another thing. We'd stopped referring to my father by either his name or any honorific. In our collective family ethos, we'd reduced him to his initials, the monogram on his old leather briefcase.

"No, for sure," my brother says in his cool way.

"I know from experience," I say. "It's so hard to see your situation from the inside. It's so hard to know that things can be different."

I want him to know we don't judge him. If he was crazy, so was I. So were all of us.

"We're here for you, Noam. We want to help you figure out a way to get out of here," my sister says.

"What do you mean?" he asks.

"You could come to Tel Aviv for a while," my sister says. "We have an extra bed. It could give you a break, a chance to clear your head."

My brother looks down and rubs the amber-colored worry beads he likes to carry on his person.

"There are lots of possibilities," I say. "You can always stay with us for a while if you don't want to be that far away."

"And do what?" he asks. But the truth was I didn't know.

"Nobody's saying it's a permanent solution," my husband says. "We're just thinking about how to get you into a different head space, so you can make good decisions about what to do next."

"I don't blame you," I say. "I know how hard it is to feel trapped in someone else's house. What about some other kind of setup?" And here I know I need to be as general as possible. "What about some kind of therapeutic environment? Someplace where you could get some counseling and support?"

"Support for what?" he asks, and I can see he is not going to make this easy. He'd admitted to us multiple times that he had a heroin problem, but now he was going to make us spell it out.

"For whatever you're struggling with," I say. "I'm not saying there's any easy fix, but as long as you're in Miami, there's no chance of anything."

"We know that; deep down, you know that," my sister says.

My brother's face is serious. "Look, you guys, I get what you're saying. And I appreciate it. I really do. But I don't see how crashing on someone's couch is going to help anything."

"Maybe not," I say. "But living with D.N.S. is definitely not going to help anything."

He keeps looking down, avoiding any of our eyes.

"It means a lot that you guys all came down," he says. "For real."

Our flight is leaving the next day at noon. We drive to my sister's place to say goodbye. She has booked her rental for another few days.

"I don't know why I did that," she says. "I wish I was leaving too."

As I take a seat, my phone rings. It's my father. He wants to say goodbye. "Well, I'm glad I got to see you at least once. I would have liked to see you more," he says.

"I'm glad I got to see you too," I say, and as I say it, I realize I mean it.

"I'm in a terrible situation. I have five children who want nothing to do with me."

"I know, Dad."

"I have seven grandchildren I never see."

"I know, Dad."

"I have nothing left, Sara. I'm all alone."

"I know, Dad."

"Was I such a terrible husband? Was I such a terrible father?"

I want to say something meaningful, something true, something that could make sense of everything that had happened, everything that was happening, and everything that would happen in the future, but my mind is blank. So I say, "I'm sorry you're suffering, Dad."

I had relied on words for so long, I'd looked to them to explain so much, but in this moment, they couldn't help me. There were no words in the world that could explain any of this. There was not a single syllable up to the task.

That night in the hotel room I take off my clothes and stand under the shower. By the time I get out, it is late. My husband is asleep. Outside the sliding glass door, I can hear the sounds of the ocean. The air-conditioning blares. I get into bed.

My husband moves toward me, but I move away. I get out of bed and find my notebook, the bound and unlined one I take with me everywhere I go, and step onto the balcony, the heavy night air.

The first thing I think when I see my father is how diminished he looks, I write. *Diminished in size, diminished in stature, diminished by illness.*

I am done writing made-up stories. Things that are true that you try to make untrue, things that are false that you try to make sound real. I've always thought that if I worked hard enough, I could write a story that someone would want to read. Now I understand that itself is a fiction. The only thing that matters now is what is in front of me. The only thing I care about now is what I can see.

13

THAT'S YOUR STORY, NOT MINE

A FEW WEEKS AFTER WE RETURNED from Miami, the hurricane hit. I'm not saying my brother's problems started with the hurricane. But after the hurricane, things got worse.

The governor was telling people to evacuate, to evacuate immediately. The hurricane was coming, and the city was running out of water, out of food. "People will die," the governor was telling people on TV. "Your children will die too."

I was several states away and texted my brother in a panic, and, somehow, he called back right away.

"Where are you?" I asked him.

"I'm driving around in the car," he said, "Looking for food. All the Walgreens are closed, Walmart, Target, every Starbucks in a ten-mile radius. Even Whole Foods is closed. They're not just closed—they're boarded up. I mean, Dad went out on Monday and bought some water and stuff, but that's already half gone."

Noam didn't sound alarmed, only mildly interested, as though he were telling a story about someone else. Obviously, my father and brother would not be evacuating; they didn't give a fuck about the governor or anyone else. Instead, they would hole up in my father's fetid studio apartment with the flickering television, but what if the power cut out, as officials promised it would? One could assume they were stocked up on drugs. I had to assume they were well prepared on that front.

I instructed my brother to keep me posted, to not let too much time pass without texting me an update. I would keep my eyes glued to my phone, I told him.

In the end, this proved unnecessary. The governor's warnings had been premature. The storm came, but nobody died. Not the parents, nor their children. There was no real damage, just some coastal flooding and overturned trees. *People will die. Your children will die too.*

Two months later, my brother tried to kill himself.

My brother is alone downstairs in my basement, which sounds worse than it is. The basement is finished, its floors covered with fake Persian rugs, its walls lined with books. I've given him a down comforter and a quilt. There is a big window next to the pull-out sofa, and the light comes in in the morning if the blinds are open. Still, he is alone in someone else's basement. He is here indefinitely. Or at least until a spot opens up at the rehab he's trying to get into.

It is night, and I hear him playing guitar. The same song he's been working on for weeks. Maybe months or years, I don't know. Some of his songs don't have words, but this one does.

> *Should I stay?*
> *Should I go?*
>
> *Who will care?*
> *Who will know?*

These are the only words to the song, as far as I can tell. The way he plays makes me want to cry. How did he learn to hold a guitar in his arms, to cradle it like a baby? I don't understand music the way he does; I don't know where it comes from.

I am folding the laundry upstairs, and through the vent, I hear him playing the same lick over and over. I thank God that he has the guitar, that it is always with him, that it is something no one can take away from him. Even if he loses this guitar, or it gets stolen, or he has to sell it, he will find his way to another guitar. This is what I tell myself to make me less afraid. All he has to do is pick one up and he is home. I know that this is true, but still I am afraid.

My husband is asleep, and my son is asleep, though he will probably be up in a couple hours, crying for his bottle or crying because he's wet or crying because he's lonely. Either my husband or I will get him what he needs, take him into bed with us, rock him, soothe him, hold him. But for now, the house is quiet.

It is almost Christmas, and the temperature is beginning to drop. Only last week, my son and I were out throwing pebbles into the creek, wearing light sweaters on a sunny day. But now the sky is bitter, the clouds heavy. My brother doesn't have a winter coat, just a flimsy beige Members Only knockoff that may or may not have belonged to my dad in the '80s. When he goes out, my brother layers a hooded sweatshirt underneath it, then puts the hood over his ears, which, along with his headphones, fulfills the dual task of keeping his ears warm while blocking out the sounds of the world.

It isn't just the winter coat. Ever since my brother arrived at our house three weeks ago, I've been in a constant state of worry. Does he have enough underwear? Is it clean? I wanted to buy him some, but I didn't know what kind he liked, and I didn't want to ask him because I didn't want to embarrass him. Instead, I bought him socks and long-sleeved T-shirts and crewneck sweaters, just as I did for my son, and casually left them on his bed, wrapped in tissue, without a word. I charged it to the credit card, even though my husband warned me we were hitting up against its limit.

"Mom, you have to buy Noam a winter coat," I told her one afternoon while slicing zucchini for a stir-fry. My mother was still living with us, as she had been since our son was born three years earlier. She was watching me cook since I preferred not to have help. Why did I have to tell her this? Why did it fall to me to point out the obvious? One obvious thing was that my brother was thirty years old; he should have been able to buy his own winter coat, but that was another story.

The dog next door starts barking, obliterating my brother's music. The dog is a Doberman pinscher; I should be used to it by now, but I'm not. The dog barks all the time. When you walk by, it comes right up close to the chain-link fence as though it's about to jump. Sometimes it tires of barking and lets out a series of sad, defeated whimpers. The neighbors across the way want to get rid of the dog. Just last week, they sent around an email with a petition for all the neighbors to sign. They want the police to come. They want the animal taken away.

I finish folding the laundry and sneak into my son's room to distribute the bounty: clean T-shirts and socks, patterned pajamas in alien and train motifs. I do an exaggerated tiptoe, terrified of waking him, but he doesn't stir. The guitar playing has stopped and, with it, my brother's singing.

In order for my brother to get into this rehab—the one in California, the one that accepts my mother's insurance—they need to know he's serious. And in order for them to know he's serious, he has to call a guy named Javier every day and tell him what's going on. My brother cannot afford to get rejected from this rehab; in the span of one month, he's already been rejected from three.

Earlier tonight, when I was taking the laundry out of the dryer, I saw him pacing back and forth, the phone cradled against his ear. "Yeah, I'm just staying by my sister," I heard him say. "It's chill." I imagine Javier as a supernatural figure, an archangel, a conduit between the earthly and the divine who held in his hands the power to grant my brother life. Now I hear my brother rummaging through his snacks, and I think about the sugar flooding his system like a drug, breaking down what little defenses he has left. In the morning, I will find the evidence all around his pull-out bed: Sour Patch Kids wrappers and Lemonheads wrappers and half-drunk plastic bottles of Dr Pepper.

I sink into the couch and stare out into space—the space that is our living room, which is not really ours. We do not own the house and only barely own its contents: the fake Persian carpets are from my in-laws' garage, the furniture bought for cheap from the previous occupant. I am tired. I should be getting ready for bed. Instead, I go to the refrigerator, inspect its contents, and begin tallying tomorrow's shopping list. *Chicken breasts, carrots, paper towels, potatoes, diapers.* My son needs feeding, and so do my husband and my brother and my mom. Every night, I make dinner for everyone—vegetable lasagna, lentil soup, chicken with lemon and garlic.

This is the woman I want to be: gracious and generous, effortless in my ability to give to my family, a woman whose home provides all who enter safe harbor. But I am not that woman. I want so badly to be her, but the harder I try, the worse I feel. My panic is worst in the morning, when I can feel it rising up like nausea, helpless to keep it from coming.

The first night he got to my house, my brother told me a story. A story about what happened when he went to my dad's apartment to get some of his stuff before he left: his favorite sweatshirt; his CD collection; some music files he had stored on my dad's computer.

When my brother got to the apartment, our father was lying naked on the bed. He was sick with cancer, yes, but apparently still very much alive. Next to him was a girl, Leah, a girl my brother knew. She had once been a congregant, a member of my father's synagogue in Miami before he was fired; she, along with her parents and older sister, came to services every Sabbath. Now she was twenty-two and lying on the bed, naked except for a pair of shorts and a bra. A copy of the Bible was open, as though they were engaged in study, which, in a sense, they were. My father was explaining to her the value of *tzedaka*—strictly translated as charity, yes, but that is only the most basic way of understanding the word. It encompasses so much more than that: the divine imperative to help someone in need. They had just finished snorting heroin, or they were about to go do more.

It wasn't the first time my brother had walked in on this scene. For the past two years, he'd been staying on and off with my dad, so he had seen this type of thing before. But that night something was different. Why is this night different from all other nights?

Because on this night, instead of getting his shit and walking out, my brother told Leah to get dressed, that he was taking her home. But before he did, he told my dad to rot in hell, and then my dad threw a phone at his head.

According to Noam, that's when my father said, "I'm going to fucking kill you."

Noam understood then that he wasn't going to be able to get his shit, that the only thing he could do was get out of there.

"C'mon, Leah," he said. "Let's go."

By then, Leah's clothes were on, and they were heading for the door, my father cursing them both.

"Don't come back," my father said.

"I'm going to rehab," Noam said.

"That's your story, not mine," my father said, and then my brother turned and walked out the door.

We are sitting on the couch in the basement. It is late, and I should be in bed. I should be fast asleep. But I cannot sleep. As long as my brother is telling this story, I cannot sleep.

"It used to be secretive. He didn't want me to know he was high. Now he just snorts in front of me. For the past six months, he's been snorting heroin out in the open." This is what my brother tells me. And it's not just heroin. It's coke, morphine, OxyContin, Dilaudid, fentanyl, crack, weed. "There's nothing I haven't been aware of him doing."

Like I said, my brother had been staying at my father's apartment, but sometimes he stayed with friends, and sometimes when he came back, the girl would be there. "Why are you even here?" my brother would say to her. "You need to get out of here." Sometimes she tells my brother she has nowhere else to go. Her mother's thrown her out, and he—my father—has a way of putting things, a way of making complicated ideas sound simple. They have good conversations, she tells him. Conversations she can't have with anyone else.

But sometimes when my brother goes to the apartment, she's in bad shape, she is losing it. Sometimes she throws herself on the floor and starts screaming, and the thing she screams is always the same, the refrain of a song, and the refrain goes like this: *Your father belongs in jail / Your father belongs in jail.* Sometimes the song has other words, words that show she understands how bad things actually are.

A girl without a family is a girl with nowhere to go. And a girl with nowhere to go has few options. My father gives her drugs. My father gives her money. Fifty dollars here, a hundred there.

A girl with nowhere to go gets herself into bad situations.

"Her last two boyfriends beat her up," my brother tells me. "And the one before that went to jail."

"So now Dad's her boyfriend?" I ask, and my brother looks at me with pity.

"You don't understand," he tells me. "Dad's not her boyfriend. He's her rabbi."

My therapist's office is a calming place. There are plants and a soft leather couch. There are mauve walls and intricate tapestries. She is not my first therapist, not by a long shot. She is one in a series of therapists, some more helpful than others, going back to when I was seventeen and looked up "psychologist" in the Yellow Pages, and drove myself into the city to see one, which I paid for with money I'd earned babysitting. I needed to talk and to find out if I was crazy. That was the summer after I graduated from high school, the summer after the winter when everything happened.

I tell my therapist about the girl, about my father, about my father and the girl.

She already knows the basic setup, but now I have more details.

"I feel like I'm going crazy," I tell her. I lean against one of her tasteful accent pillows and eye the afghan on her armchair.

She gives her concerned look and uncrosses her ankles. I stare at her block-heeled European shoes.

"You're not crazy," she says. "You're holding a lot."

"I feel like I'm supposed to be Ellis Island," I say. "Like I'm supposed to welcome in all the refugees from my fallen-apart family."

She nods and makes her sympathetic face. "And that's difficult for you," she says. "To feel you must be the responsible one. That somehow, it always falls to you."

I tell her about lying in bed at night, listening to the front door open, the sounds of my brother going outside. Maybe he is stepping out for a joint or for a cigarette, or maybe he is simply planning to take a walk in the freezing night air in his wafer-thin jacket. But another possibility is that he is planning to turn left onto Elm Avenue and take it all the way down until he reaches the Metro station, where he will hop on an inbound train to the city, where he can get anything he wants.

"What are you afraid of?" she asks.

I was afraid of the obvious things. Death, drugs, police. But I was also afraid of the neighbors. We'd been living here, in this nice Maryland suburb, for just over a year, having moved for my husband's job to a place full of young children and two-car garages. There was no room for a strange man walking around with headphones with nowhere to go. I remind my therapist that, when we first moved in, we'd received a visit from the city-code enforcer, informing us there'd been an anonymous tip: we'd allowed our trash bins to linger too long at the curb after the weekly collection. "Unless it's pickup day," the code enforcer told me, "they cannot be visible from the street." Until that moment, I didn't know there was a city-code enforcer. What else did he enforce?

"I may be paranoid," I say to my therapist, "but I don't think our neighbors like us."

She gives her puzzled look. "Why wouldn't they like you?"

"How should I know? Maybe because we're Jewish." I am only partially joking.

"Is that a concern for you?" She does her inquisitive face.

I tell her about the Christmas decoration in the house across from ours. It wasn't just some twinkling lights or candy canes staked in the lawn. It was a red strobe light emanating from the heart of the house, soaking everything in crimson. Even with our shades closed, the red seeped through, like blood or the flashing of an ambulance siren.

We talk about this for a while, and then my time is up, and I don't feel any better except for the fact that I've gotten out of the house with a clear destination in mind, with a specific place I have to be at a certain time, to talk to someone who asks me questions that have no answers and then charges me for the privilege. She is probably the least helpful therapist I'd ever had, but I keep seeing her because it makes me feel like I am doing something, and because the thought of trying to find another one is exhausting.

"Life's difficult for you," she says as I'm about to leave. As though it's breaking news. As though I didn't know.

I remember a time when I used to pray. Sometimes for hours. Today there is no possibility of prayer. I have left religion and have nothing to replace it with.

This year, Christmas and Hanukkah would fall on the same night, a rare occurrence that had to do with the movement of planets, the lunar and solar calendars colliding. The holidays were coming for us; I knew because of the art projects my son brought home from preschool: Christmas trees made of popsicle sticks, snowmen born from cotton balls, even a watercolor dreidel to show they were inclusive. Tonight is the Winter Wonderland recital. My husband has to work, and my mother's out of town, so I go by myself, the only face my son will spot in the crowd.

The recital is scheduled for 5:00, and because it is winter, it is nearly dark as I walk up the hill to the school. I do not expect to be nervous, but I am. I have never done this before. Until he started going to school, my son was just a baby. Now he is a person—a person with his nose painted red, wearing a reindeer hat made of construction paper.

When he sees me, he calls out, "Mommy!" and for a minute, I think he will break ranks, but he is old enough to know the Winter Wonderland recital is serious business, and after waving to me, he sits back down and awaits instruction.

The school's director calls for everyone to take their seats, but parents keep arriving—more parents than seem commensurate with the number of students, more parents than one can imagine. Those lucky enough to have found seats are packed together on tiny plastic chairs meant for three-year-olds. The kids are getting restless; a few begin to cry, and their parents call out reassurances from across the room. The air inside is warm and getting warmer. "Can we open a window?" someone asks, but the school is housed in an aging three-story house, its windows painted shut due to county lead regulations.

Finally, the children begin to sing. *Dashing through the snow / In a one-horse open sleigh / O'er the fields we go / Laughing all the way* . . . When they reach the chorus, they all shake their jingle bells. I crane my neck to get a better look at Jonah, who is dutifully singing the words and jingling his bells at all the right parts, a focused look on his face.

By now, the room is so packed I think I might pass out. I need some fresh air, but parents are blocking me on every side. When I look to the doorways, they are blocked too. I am trapped.

In the meantime, the songs keep coming. *Then one shiny Christmas Eve, Santa came to say* . . . All around me parents hold their iPhones aloft like torches. Some rush to the front and adopt a crouching position, contorting to get a better angle. I snap away on my Android to prove I love my child. Now the teachers are leading the kids in a new Yuletide favorite: *I have a little dreidel, I made it out of clay* . . .

Then, all of a sudden, there is a big "HO HO HO" in a deep-throated voice and the presence of a large man with a shiny black belt. "Santa!" the teachers squeal, as though in surprise. The kids meld into a mosh pit of frenzied screams. "*Who wants a present from Santa?*" the man bellows, and the kids go berserk. "*One at a time!*" Santa says. He begins to call out names, one by one, and each time he does, a child rushes to the front of the room, and Santa hands them a small, wrapped parcel from his sack.

The room, once stuffy, is now sweltering, the radiators in overdrive, parents sweating in patented lightweight down. I have already shed my hat and gloves and scarf and jacket and sweater; there is nothing left for me to shed. The heat starts in my chest and moves up to my face. There is a pain in the back of my throat, making it hard to swallow. Until this moment, I have never seen Santa up close. One thing I had always respected about him was how discreet he was—leaving gifts by the fireplace, then disappearing up the chimney out of sight. Now here he is, his old-man feet in black orthopedics, the pilling red suit straining against his girth. It is one thing for my son to sing festive wintery songs with his classmates; it is something else entirely to come face to face with the corporeality of Saint Nick.

The kids are called up in a succession that never seems to end. *Morgan, Madigan, Kendall, Jackson, Zachary.* When my son's name is called, he walks up to Santa, eyes glazed, as though in a trance, and holds out his hand to get his present. "Say 'Thank you, Santa,'" his teacher instructs, and he does as he is told. *No!* I want to scream. *Turn around, give it back! We don't take presents from men in shiny black belts! This isn't what we believe in!*

The obvious question is why we didn't send our child to a Jewish school; there were several within driving distance, and Jonah could have spent the holiday season singing songs about the Maccabees and learning about the miracle of the oil that lasted eight days instead of only one because God makes miracles for the Jewish people, which we sing about every night of Hannukah, just after we light the candles—

My son could be learning about his own God, his own people's story of salvation instead of singing songs about an imaginary man in a red suit, but he wasn't, and that was because I had made a promise to myself long ago. After what I'd seen, I could never send my child to a Jewish school. I could not pass down the thing I loved because it had hurt me too much.

It is not a white Christmas; it is a Christmas of freezing rain. I know because we are driving around in it, on our way to the nearest urgent care, or at least the nearest one that's open.

"I told you that you should've gotten a flu shot," my husband says.

Ever since I returned home from the Winter Wonderland recital, I'd been marooned in bed, head pounding, throat sore, a low fever moving in and out with my dreams. By now, it had been four days. In this state, I was unable to care for my child, making me a failure as a woman and a mother. My husband had been doing everything, and he was fried.

But that was not the only thing. When we moved here for his new job, we'd shipped furniture and dishes and books and clothes—our whole lives—in a 1,000-cubic-foot shipping container. We signed a one-year lease and bought a used car, but by now it was clear this job would not last. The way my husband had described his last conversation with his boss, a small, weasel-like man of limited intelligence, it was clear the man despised him. I'd like to say I handled this news calmly, that I took my husband's hand and told him everything was going to be okay, but that is not what happened. Instead, I said, "You're about to get fired?" and he said, "I'm not going to get fired." And I said, "Of course you're about to be fired! I can't believe this."

It was the only thing I could say. I couldn't help it. I had no net, no resting point; my brain delivered me straight to the worst possible thing that could happen.

"Do you not remember me asking you to get a flu shot?" my husband asks now, and I say nothing.

"*I* got a flu shot, we made sure our *son* got a flu shot. I'm just trying to understand why you think it doesn't apply to you."

"Oh, but you're an expert at taking care of yourself," I say.

I had read self-help books and met with therapists and seen couples' counselors, but the only reliable thing I knew about marriage was how to fight.

"Don't make this about me," my husband says. "Why can't you take some responsibility?"

It is Christmas, and the streets are empty. The only people out are desperate people, desperate for milk or cigarettes or Chinese food or gas or medical care. We fell into the latter category, but it hardly mattered; if you are driving around in the freezing rain on Christmas Day, you will feel unhinged.

"Take some responsibility? Are you fucking kidding me?" I say. "In case you haven't noticed, I am the responsible one."

There is something about my husband's face when it hardens, when he morphs into a person I can neither move nor access, that makes it impossible to stay inside my body. It comes on slowly and also suddenly: the instant lightness, the numbness that starts in my extremities, the absolute necessity of escape, followed by the near-simultaneous awareness that I am in a moving vehicle and there is nowhere to go.

It is the knowledge that I am trapped, even as we drive at high speed down the near-empty highway, that sets something loose. It is here that I start screaming, screaming without words. I scream at the top of my lungs. I scream because I am angry, and because I no longer care. I scream because I am mad at my mother and mad at my brother and mad at my husband and mad at God and mad at myself. The car speeds through the pouring rain, the windshield wipers going *swish, swish, swish*, just like they do in the song I sing to my son every night. In the back seat, the car seat is empty. My son is at my in-laws' house so he cannot hear me screaming. Nobody can hear me screaming. Our car is a capsule spinning through space, outside of time, outside of reality.

My husband lurches toward me and the car swerves. "*What is wrong with you?*" he yells. "You want me to have an accident? Is that what you want?"

I crumple in the seat and try to focus on the shards of rain as they hit the car, but still I cannot stop the tears from coming.

My husband wants me to go on some kind of medication—Xanax or Valium or lorazepam or Klonopin, anything legal that will quiet me down. I was already taking 75 mg of sertraline (brand name, Zoloft), but apparently it wasn't enough. I could still feel.

Finally, we reach the urgent care. The doctor comes in to poke and prod and swab. I am diagnosed with strep and prescribed antibiotics, fluids, and rest.

"I have another question," I say. "Umm, well, I've been under a lot of stress lately. Actually, not just lately, but more in general. But there's also this specific situation. My brother tried to kill himself—and he couldn't stay where he was living because he was living with my dad, and my dad would have killed him. So now he's living with us, but we don't know if he's going to get into this rehab or not—"

And here my voice cracked, and the sadness started seeping out. No doctor wants to see that. Within seconds, he is writing out another prescription: 25 mg of Xanax, to be taken as needed.

We stop off at the pharmacy on the way home, where we buy a bottle of water, and I take it right there in the car. My husband was right. It quiets me down immediately. It's so easy and straightforward I wonder what I was ever afraid of. I lean my head against the car window and stare off into the horizon, an ever-expanding highway.

When we get home, I take off my clothes and get into bed. My husband comes in and takes off his boots.

"I can't move," I tell him. "I can't do anything."

"Just rest," he says.

"You're in charge of the baby," I tell him. "You're in charge of everything."

I look at the clock. I am neither asleep nor awake. The darkness of the room is total. It hurts to swallow, but my mind spins round and round. Did I sleep the whole night? Was it still afternoon? I have the feeling of coming to from a series of dreams, all of them in fragments, which my brain tries and fails to piece together.

In the heavy silence, I can feel the house is empty, and it takes me a minute to place where everyone is. I remember that my husband and my son and my brother are at my in-laws', where my husband's siblings and their kids converge every Christmas to watch television on their big-screen TV and consume highly processed foods.

With a light buzz, my phone illuminates the darkness. It's a message from my sister-in-law: a picture of my son at my in-laws' house. He is lying on my niece's lap, stretched out in front of the fireplace, drinking his bottle. It looks like a magazine ad. He is able to make himself comfortable wherever he goes. But what about my brother? I imagine him in my in-laws' family room, the giant-screen TV always humming in the background, the faux fire in the faux fireplace, the influx of holiday-themed snacks, the red cardboard take-out cups, the chatter about the next day's sales—I could see how it could all be too much for him.

I worry about my brother being bored. I worry about him being depressed. I worry about something terrible happening, as though so many terrible things hadn't already happened. I want my mom here to make sure everything's okay, but my mother isn't here because she is in New York with her boyfriend, Jim, celebrating Christmas with Jim's daughter. I didn't want my mom to go. I begged her not to go. But she was starting her new life and did not care what I wanted.

I must have fallen asleep again because I wake into the darkness. This time the sheets are soaking, and I am covered in a cold, wet sweat.

My phone beeps and glows with the light and sound of another message. Ruby is all over Noam, my sister-in-law texts. Ruby is my three-year-old niece. Another message: Olive likes him too! Olive is my ten-year-old niece. It's nuts. She likes almost no one.

This is the real Noam, I think to myself, the Noam to whom women, children, and animals were hopelessly drawn, any creature that could sniff out goodness.

I'm sorry, I text my husband. I'm sorry for acting so crazy.

I'm sorry too, he texts back. It won't always be like this.

It's the morning of New Year's Eve when I tell Noam we are going on an adventure, just the two of us.

We walk into town, and I take his arm as we cross the street and step into Polly Sue's, a thrift shop filled with mannequins wearing evening gowns from the '40s and '50s, cases of costume jewelry, and pillbox hats with netting. There is a long rack of men's winter coats, divided by size, each marked with a tag announcing its decade.

"These are all half-price today," the saleslady tells us.

"We're buying you a winter coat, and that's that," I tell him. "Don't even say anything, because it's already happening."

He tries a military-style fatigue jacket, a navy three-quarter-length wool coat with leather buttons, a plaid jacket with big pockets.

"What about that one?" I ask, looking up at one of the displays.

The saleslady takes it down for us, and my brother slips it on. It is dark gray wool lined with soft gray shearling, and it hangs perfectly on his frame. He looks at himself in the mirror, buttons it up to the top, and puts on his sunglasses.

"What do you think?" he asks me, and I tell him the truth. "I think you look hot."

I'm upstairs folding laundry when I hear the sounds of my brother's guitar. In two days, he will get on a plane to California. The melody he is playing does not have words. It is like light on the surface of water.

I stop folding, walk downstairs, and sit on his bed. The sheets are covered with blue pen marks and sweat marks, the arts section of the Sunday paper, and a 758-page biography of Rasputin.

"I like what you're playing," I say. "It's beautiful."

"Thanks," he says and stops playing.

"No, don't stop," I say.

On both my mother's and my father's side, we are descended from the Levites, the tribe that played music in the Holy Temple in Jerusalem, when such a thing still stood. It was the sacred duty of the Levites to play music—the flute, the harp, the lute—and to sing. They filled the Temple choirs; dozens and dozens of them, their voices carried up to heaven on the tendrils of incense and sacrificial smoke.

When the Temple was destroyed, there was nowhere left for the Levites to sing, to play their stringed instruments. There was nowhere left for the people to bring their offerings to God, to make a pilgrimage three times a year to dance and worship and sprinkle frankincense over a burnt-goat offering that they would feast upon with their families in celebrations that lasted for days. God was evicted; there was no home to go back to.

I am thinking about all the times my brother played music for me. The time when he was only seventeen and my mother's friend Joanna's husband died and he wrote a song about it, maybe one of the first songs he'd ever written, and when he played it, you felt that it was just like Joanna's husband, that he wouldn't want you to feel bad for him, bad that he died; or the time Jeremy and I spent Thanksgiving at my parents' house, when such a thing still stood, and Noam and Ephraim were still living there. Before dinner, Ephraim sat at the piano, Noam sat on the couch with his guitar, and my mom took her place in the big wing chair in the corner, still with her apron on, singing harmony. I don't remember what song they were singing, but I remember I felt grateful to be sitting in that house, that this was my family, that these men with green eyes and overgrown facial hair, these men who played music and had holes in their sweaters, these were my brothers.

I can feel my face collapsing in on itself, the burning behind my eyes, and then they come, all the tears in a rush, and I bury my head in my hands.

"Do you need a hug?" my brother asks, and I move the laptop sitting between us, and throw my arms around him and hold on. I can feel the sobbing moving through me like a current, something I think at first that maybe I can stop, but soon it is clear I cannot. I am getting his shirt wet, and also the T-shirt underneath his shirt, the T-shirt I had bought for him, the one he was too embarrassed to thank me for.

I don't let go, and neither does he.

14

ONE LITTLE GOAT

'TWAS THE MORNING BEFORE PASSOVER, and I am stressed out of my mind. Yes, the brisket is made and also the charoset. So is the carrot kugel and the chicken soup and matzo balls. But there is still so much to do: boil the eggs, roast the shankbone, rinse the bunches of parsley and store them in paper towel–lined ziplock bags. The silverware still needed to be polished, and so did the candlesticks. The following night, seventeen people would be sitting down to Seder at our home, eighteen if my father-in-law's colleague who'd been invited at the last minute decided to join us. The folding table needed to be picked up from my in-laws', along with the folding chairs, and placed in our living room, where the story of our enslavement and subsequent exodus would unfold.

But instead of doing any of this, I am crouched down on the kitchen floor, phone pressed hot to my ear.

It's Leah on the phone. How can I describe who she is to me, how I know her? Let's call her the girl my father hurt. That's one way to put it.

"Your father ruined my life," she's telling me. "My mom got papers from court to put me in a mental hospital."

I don't know what to say, so I say, "I just want to listen. I want to understand what's happening."

I know the basic facts. She is twenty-two. She has a boyfriend, but she can't always stay with him. She has a mother, but she can't always stay with her. And so, on the nights when she has nowhere to go, she stays with my father in his airless studio apartment. This arrangement had been going on for months, maybe years. But now she is upset. Something has happened.

"He threw a cell phone at my toe. My toenail came off. He put me in the hospital."

Her words are coming out clipped and fast, in a rush of broken pieces. When I first found out her name, some months earlier, I'd looked her up on the Internet and studied her face. It was nothing like mine, but that, I understood, was only a technicality. This girl, this stranger, knows my father in a way that only a daughter can.

"Hold on," she tells me, and I can hear a woman screaming in the background. The phone drops, and there is more noise, Leah yelling back. There is the sound of furniture moving, or doors closing, I can't tell what exactly, and then she gets back on the phone. "Here, talk to my mom," she says. "Maybe she'll listen to you."

The voice of an older woman comes on the line. She is already speaking, she is already mid-sentence, her pitch rising. She knows who I am, the daughter of the man who did this to her daughter. And so there is no need to stand on ceremony, no need to say hello or introduce herself; we can dispense with formalities here, we both know what's what. I can feel her veins throbbing through the phone, across the states that separate us. "My life has been completely destroyed by this so-called rabbi!" she screams. "And she refuses to press charges!"

I cannot make out precisely what she says next, but I understand that she is reviewing the facts as she knows them, going back to the first night it happened—the first, but not last, time she found her daughter at the rabbi's apartment. Like her daughter, she speaks quickly, so quickly I struggle to scribble down her words, coming at me in a torrent I cannot staunch: "*She was there until two in the morning. . . . Your father put five hundred dollars in her purse. . . . The police investigator got bribed too . . .*"

At this insinuation, I can hear Leah, who is apparently standing right next to her mother, scream, "*You took money from the rabbi too!*"

At this, her mother screams something back, and then Leah commandeers the phone again. "She was the one who gave the rabbi my number in the first place," she says, and her mother mutters something in her defense, something I can barely hear, then says she's done; she's walking away.

Leah lowers her voice. "I can't go home because my mom will just keep trying to put me in a mental hospital. But I won't go because I'm not crazy."

"You're not crazy," I say. "You're a victim."

This was before I learned that you weren't supposed to say "victim"—you were supposed to say "survivor," as if saying the word could make it true.

"Okay. But how does that help me? It's Passover, and I have nowhere to go."

I want to do something for her, but I don't know what. Am I supposed to invite her to my home? Even if she started driving now, even if she drove through the night, she wouldn't arrive for days. Should I buy her a plane ticket? A train ticket? What do I owe her?

There is more noise. Her mother is screaming something, but I can't hear what.

"Sara," she says, out of breath, "I'll have to call you back."

Then there is just the silence of the phone, dead without her voice to animate it.

I start shaking, sitting there holding the phone. Or maybe I'd been shaking all along and am just now noticing it. I sit there on the floor and close my eyes. I want to walk out the door and keep walking. I want to walk and walk and walk until I can't walk anymore. Eventually though, I would have to stop. That was the problem. Even if I vanished, I needed somewhere to go.

A few minutes later, there is a flutter of texts, delivered at lightning speed.

> My mom is at the court paying for a new marchman act
> so I can be sent to a crazy place.
> Do you have a family lawyer?
> I need help.
> I am NOT asking for money. I'm asking for help.
> I am just 22.

Then, another text. This time a picture. A selfie of her and her boyfriend posing for the camera, him in reflective aviator sunglasses and a white tank top.

> This kid is all I have, and he is 26 and lives with his
> mother that doesn't always let me sleep there.

I imagine how she might imagine me. With my fancy education and my nice husband and my young son. If you Googled me, these facts made themselves known. I could see how, taken together, they might form a picture of the kind of person I knew myself not to be:

someone lucky, someone who had their shit together. Was this how she saw me? As someone who couldn't imagine what it was like to be her? I wonder if, in her mind, I had crossed some kind of bridge, some kind of bridge to the other side of suffering.

I tell her I will do some research, to see if I can find any local resources that could help her. I can't make any promises, I tell her, but I will try.

Thank you. As long as you believe that I am not crazy
and if you speak to the judge or whoever I get fucked
over with next by my mother,
then I might have a chance,
but I can't be locked away for Passover.
Can you research a marchman act?
The doctor deemed me mentally stable and said this
was not the place for me, and I signed a paper and he
let me go.

I think of what my mother said the last time I tried to talk to her about this. "There is such a thing as real evil in this world. People don't want to believe it, but it's true."

I text Leah back that I am sorry, sorry about everything. I wish there was more I could do. That's what I tell her. Here's another thing I write: Stay away from him, and I use my father's name. You need to stay away from him, I tell her. If you want to be free, that is what you have to do.

It wasn't my first time hosting the Seder at our home. When we lived in Jerusalem, we'd invited our friends and their children, who fell asleep on their parents' laps as we drank all four cups and talked into the night. Since moving back to America—not just to America, but to the most American of states, just outside Washington, DC, where my husband grew up and where we'd been living for the past two years—we continued having Passover at our house. It was the one holiday that still felt important, the one holiday whose meticulous observances still bound me.

But this was the first year it felt like something I had to do rather than something I wanted to do. Another thing in my life whose primary purpose was to generate lists—who is coming, what to buy, what to cook, where to seat everyone. My brother Ephraim was coming in with his wife and twins from Chicago, my mother- and father-in-law would be arriving from their nice suburb thirty minutes away, forty-five with traffic, my sister- and brother-in-law and niece and nephew, who lived down the street from my in-laws, would be there too, and so would my mother and her boyfriend.

My mother was still living with us, though she was spending more and more time with Jim, a soft-spoken man with a named chair at a small but respectable university whom she met online one year ago. At first, they went out only on Saturday nights. Then she started spending the weekend there. Then the weekend started expanding, from Thursday afternoon to Monday morning. At the moment, she was here to help me prepare for the Seder.

I was exhausted, even though I had no right to be. This was the first year of my life I didn't do the full Passover preparations, only the bare minimum, removing all bread and crackers and pasta from my home, wiping down the pantry shelves. I was trying to make my life easier, but somehow it felt too easy—like I was getting away with something I didn't want to get away with. Like I was trying to trick God.

I am standing in front of an open cabinet, looking at my wineglasses, when my mom comes in. Glass is not like other materials like wood or pottery or stone. Even though it's translucent, its surface is impenetrable, which means that objects made from glass can be used on Passover, as long as they are soaked first in boiling water for twenty-four hours. I stare at the glasses. I will have to arrange a series of boiling pots and fill tubs with water and rotate them overnight.

"What should I do?" I ask my mom. For some reason, I still feel I need her permission.

"Are you crazy?" she says. "Don't even think about it."

Then she adds: "It's okay with God, believe me."

We do not talk about the fact that, every year for thirty years, my mother began her Passover preparations six weeks in advance. It wasn't enough to simply clear the home of leavened foods, as the Torah commanded. The pantry and refrigerator had to be emptied of all contents, wiped clean, lined with foil. The cabinets, the countertops, the kitchen table, the stove, the oven, the sink—all had to be sanitized. In the days leading up the Seder night, my mother would awake in the middle of the night after a few hours' sleep to pour boiling water over the countertops before covering them with contact paper. Only then would she begin cooking, the foamy, eggy smell of boiling matzah balls mixing with my dreams and dragging me from sleep.

How does one remove even the possibility of the possibility that a breadcrumb might still be lurking somewhere? There was no way to know. And that was why, the night before the Seder, after all the pantry shelves and countertops had been relined, after every part of the house had been swept, vacuumed, dusted, and laundered, we took a wooden spoon and a feather and turned off all the lights and walked, together, my mother, my father, me, my sister and my three little brothers, through our house, from room to room, searching for something, anything, that we'd forgotten—some crumb, some speck, some infinitesimal piece of matter that we had, in our carelessness, overlooked. In this quest, we asked God to help us, to render any leaven still within our possession, whether we'd seen it or not, whether we knew about it or not, whether we'd removed it or not, annulled and ownerless, like the dust of the earth.

My mother didn't care about any of this anymore, which made me wonder why I still did. But the decision would have to wait; it was nearly three o'clock, and I had to pick up my son from school.

The air is fresh and clear, and people outside are planting flowers in their yards. My son's school is only a ten-minute walk from our house, just through the park and over a wooden foot-bridge, and my mom decides to join me. It is obviously, defiantly spring, the season I hate most—the hesitant, creeping warmth, the in-between-ness of it.

My mother is telling me about a cherry-blossom festival, the one Jim is taking her to in a few days.

"Mom, I've been talking to Leah."

I do not know I am going to say these words until they come out of my mouth.

"Who?"

"*Lay-ahh*," I say again, stretching out each syllable. "You know, *Leah*? Remember her?"

Of course my mother remembers her. She used to see her at synagogue every week. Her parents had been members of my father's congregation, back when he still had a congregation.

They came every Shabbat to sing, to pray, to hear the Torah portion chanted aloud. Of course my mother remembered her. It was my mother, after all, who'd received a call on her cell phone at two in the morning from the lobby of the apartment building where she lived with my father. Except that, by the time she received that call, my mother no longer lived there. She'd left with a small suitcase a month earlier and gone to Nova Scotia to stay with my brother. But the security guard didn't know that. He was calling because it was 2:00 a.m. and there was a woman standing in front of him screaming that her daughter was upstairs in the rabbi's apartment and no one was answering the landline, and this was the only other number they had on file.

"Did you really not know?"

I knew it wasn't the right time to ask this question, a question I had asked before. But this question, like so many other questions, was my vice; I couldn't stop myself from asking.

"I didn't know," she says.

"Do you promise?"

"Yes."

"Do you swear to God?"

"I swear to God."

"But how? How could you not know?"

I know I should have stopped, but I couldn't, or maybe I didn't want to. I was tired of being the only one who was angry.

"If you ask me this one more time, I'm going to go crazy! I mean it. I can't take this anymore!"

My mother is screaming in the middle of the street, and she doesn't care who hears.

"Okay, okay," I say. "Calm down, I believe you."

"Don't you dare tell me to calm down!" she screams. "You think you're the only one who can feel things?" She grabs her purse from underneath the empty stroller and starts to walk away.

"Where are you going?" I call after her, but she just shakes her head and keeps walking until she disappears from view.

It's late afternoon, and the sun is high in the sky, the trees still bare, some with pubescent buds. Without their leaves, the trees offer no protection, and the sun beats down on my face, and my head begins to pound. I am supposed to be on my way to pick up my child. A few minutes ago, everything was fine, and then suddenly it is not, because I cannot be quiet, I cannot keep myself from picking a scab until it bleeds.

I need to sit down, but there is nowhere to sit. I need to drink water, but I've forgotten to bring any. School isn't out yet, and the streets are still quiet, void of children. I think of returning home, but the distance seems too great, the sun too bright. Besides, it's almost three o'clock; my son is waiting for me. I keep walking, but I can feel myself, the self that is me, detaching from my physical self, going somewhere else entirely.

It is here that I get the idea that I cannot walk to my son's preschool and I cannot walk home, that I cannot do anything except make things worse, and it is this thought that causes the panic to take over. It used to be that my panic attacks came only once in a while, but now they happen all the time, and I don't know how to stop them. Where is my agency? Where is my effort, my diligence, to get better? It is this thought that breeds a new panic—the panic that I am not doing enough to rid myself of the panic. This panic layers itself nicely on top of the original panic, but not before being blanketed by another layer of panic—the panic that I am on my way to pick up my son from school and I am failing even in this simple task, at this most basic requirement of motherhood.

I have the familiar, unbearable urge to cut into my flesh, to run a dull blade against the soft skin of my forearm, a habit I've developed in recent years. But I don't have anything sharp with me, and soon the park will fill with children, children running to the slides and swings, so happy that they don't even know they are happy. I need to be discreet, and so I take the nail of my right index finger and press it into the underbelly of my arm until I break the skin. The pain is sharp and clear, eclipsing anything else, and for a moment, there is only the pleasure of its immediacy until I look down and wonder what I've done.

There, staring back at me, is a raised and ragged cherry half-moon, still in its earliest incarnation, just beginning to bloom. I cross the bridge and turn right into the park, surprised to see that there's a water fountain up ahead; I must have passed it a thousand times, but I'd never noticed it before. Like a child, I lean over and take long, gurgling sips, the water cold and metal-lic. There's a creek that runs the length of the park and, just at the moment that I look up, the sun hits the water in a way that scatters the light in a thousand different directions, creating tiny prisms of color.

In my mind's eye, I can see how all this could go down—a slow or sudden disintegration, the gradual abnegation of maternal duties. If I really wanted to disappear, I could.

Are you breathing? The question comes to me out of nowhere, a refrain from my old therapist. There's a bench, and I sit down for a minute. I force myself to take a breath. Then I start pushing the empty stroller up the hill.

∽

A few days later, I am on my way to pick up my son from school when my phone rings. I swipe "reject call," and a second later, there's a text, followed by another, and another, then another.

> Sara
> I have 50$ to my name
> I'm homeless for tonight
> My fiancés mom hit me today

Her texts erupt like poems, misshapen haikus about all the darkness in the world just sitting there, right below the surface. She was always talking about how she needed to get a paper, a paper to show to the court that would prove she needed therapy because of "what Danny did to me." She referred to my father not only by his first name, but by his childhood diminutive. She was always referencing the judge, her lawyer, a missing $300, but the details kept moving around. Some days her mother was the only one who cared; other days she was deliberately trying to drive her insane.

"There will always be someone to save and fix," my therapist says. "It's not your job to save them or fix it. You need to keep healthy boundaries."

I am seeing a new therapist. Actually, not a new therapist, but the old therapist I used to see before I started seeing the new one, whom I had decided to stop seeing after she suggested I wear a rubber band on my wrist and snap it if I felt a panic attack coming on.

"She has no one," I tell him. "Nothing."

"She is an adult," he says. "She is capable of helping herself. But she needs professional help for that. You are not equipped to be her therapist. Your job is to take care of yourself."

"I feel like I need to do something for her."

"Then help her get information to help herself. You are not a savior."

A few days later, I send Leah a text.

> Leah, I really want to help you, but these issues you are
> struggling with are far beyond what I can do. It is clear
> to me that what you need is some professional help . . .
> NOT because you are crazy, but because of the terrible
> ways you have been hurt. I am going to forward you a
> couple links . . . they can offer you legal and psychological
> help that I cannot.

I text her the phone numbers of two domestic violence shelters near her. This enrages her. I've insulted her. And like a caged animal, she bares her claws.

> Your dad is the only person that ever hurt me

Your dad. In this case, she does not use his name or its diminutive. *Your dad.* That's what she says, and she says it for a reason. Just by virtue of being his child, I bear the clammy film of complicity. She knows it, and I know it. This time, I do not respond.

As always, there is more to buy; there is always more to buy. The Seder is tonight, but still there is more to buy. I give my husband a list, but I know I am probably forgetting something, and anyway I've been cooking all morning, and I need a reason to get out of the house. We go to the store together, an occurrence so rare it's almost transgressive.

My phone is making little noises, the way it does when it has something to tell me. I was getting a message, then another.

"Shit," I say.

"What is it?" my husband asks.

"I didn't want to tell you."

"Tell me what?"

"Leah's been trying to get in touch with me."

"Leah who?"

"*Leah*," I say. How was I supposed to describe her? What was I supposed to call her? You know, Leah, the girl my father abused once his own daughters were gone and he still needed someone to abuse?

I saw that he realized then who I was talking about.

"Since when?"

"I don't know. A day or two, maybe."

"And you didn't write her back?"

"I just can't deal with it at the moment."

"I don't get it. I thought it was you who wanted to talk to her."

"I did. I do. But I just can't—"

"Can't what?"

And without realizing it, the words come out of my mouth, words I didn't know I was going to say until I say them. "I'm ashamed."

"Ashamed of what?"

"Because I'm his daughter. Because I am like him. Because I am sick and broken and dangerous." I couldn't believe I had to explain this.

"No," he says.

"Don't you get it?" I say. "I'm his blood. Everything about me is tainted."

"No," he says.

Only years later will I come to understand the burden this placed on my husband. How could I expect him to understand what I was talking about?

"Do you think I want to be thinking about this?" I ask him. "Do you think this is what I want to be thinking about? Don't you think I would rather be thinking about redecorating?"

"You should write that down," he says.

"Good idea," I say.

"I'm serious," he says. "You should write all of this down. If you don't, it's going to kill you."

It is Seder night, and my mother-in-law comes bearing aloft a flourless chocolate cake, chocolate-chip meringues, a checker-board sponge cake, jelly cookies as crumbly as sand. My sister- and brother-in-law and niece and nephew bring crayons and coloring books for my son and gallons of grape juice. My father-in-law's colleague comes with shrink-wrapped boxes of Kosher-for-Passover chocolate-covered marshmallows and chewy jelly rings. My mother's boyfriend, Jim, walks in with a bouquet of flowers and a bottle of wine. "This one's just for you," he says with a wink as he hands me the bottle.

My husband leads us through the recitation of the kiddush, the ritual washing of hands, the eating of the parsley dipped in salt water, parsley to remind us of spring, salt water to remind us of tears. We eat the bitter herbs that symbolize the bitterness of our enslavement and eat our matzah, sometimes referred to as the bread of affliction, sometimes as the bread of freedom.

My mother is sitting next to me, and next to her is Jim. The fact that he is not Jewish would have been shocking if we still had the ability to be shocked. His arm is around my mother's shoulders, which is even more shocking; in nearly four decades of marriage, I'd never seen my father do that.

He smiles at my mom and squeezes her shoulder. She looks at him and smiles back, like they're in high school. I like Jim, but he is a newcomer. He knows my mother left an abusive marriage, but he has no idea how bad things actually were, how bad things still are.

I look at Ephraim, seated two seats away. His wedding, nearly four years earlier, seems like a lifetime ago. Now his twin two-year-olds are sitting next to him, his daughter to his right, his son to his left, his wife next to their son. She is telling him, "No, there are no cars at the table. No, there are no trucks." He starts to cry. "Ephraim, can you deal with this?" she says.

My brother's looking straight ahead. He is still wearing his sunglasses, although it's night and we're indoors. I know he is a good dad, but I can see he is exhausted. I look at my sister-in-law, who is seven years his senior. I could understand why he married someone older. He wanted to be taken care of. But now there is too much for her to take care of. I look at her. Her glasses are smeared with a greasy film, and her bra strap is slipping. She picks up her wineglass and drains it.

My brother takes his son, Gideon, on his lap, and the boy's mood changes instantly. Now he is smiling, while Ephraim bounces him up and down on his knee.

Tired of bouncing, Gideon starts crying again, and Ephraim looks at his wife. "I think he wants you," he says and hands the baby over the table, Gideon's little feet briefly dangling over the wineglasses.

"That's convenient," she says. She takes the baby and looks away.

I wanted to talk to Ephraim, to tell him everything. But he had made it clear to me on more than one occasion that he could not afford to spend any time thinking or talking about anything related to our father. He had his wife and kids to think of, he told me the last time I tried to broach the topic. "I have to be in my life" were the exact words he used.

Finally, it's time to eat. Everything else had changed, but the food was the same: the beets boiled and grated by hand, then mixed with horseradish root, the brisket surrounded by potatoes and carrots, the matzah kugel studded with apples.

After the meal, it's time to sing, but I cannot sing the songs of Passover without thinking of my father.

In the days leading up to the Seder, my father would listen to music from Jerusalem—one album in particular, recorded by his friends from the yeshiva on Mount Zion, when all the disaffected young Jewish men who had long hair and hated the war came to Jerusalem to find themselves or to find God, whichever happened first.

You knew my father was preparing for the Seder because he would go downstairs, take the album out of its tissue-paper sleeve, and play "Ki Lo Na'eh, Ki Lo Ya'eh" ("Because it is proper for Him, because it befits Him)" on the record player, the banjos and electric fiddles filling the air. With this song, the holiness of Jerusalem entered our home, and my father changed; moving about the house with lightness and a sense of purpose, he began to gently unpack the Haggadot from the cardboard boxes they sat in all year long, placing one at each guest's place.

A simple melody set against the beating of a hand drum, the song kept growing—violins, horns, a staccato drumbeat, all extolling the wonder of God—

> *Yours alone is the world,*
> *God, for all in the world is Yours.*

The lyrics moved through the rooms of our house, through the organs of my body, filling everything with light. The joy of praising God was the joy of being alive. The joy of praising God was a joy that knew no bounds. The joy of praising God is not the afterthought of gratitude. It is the thing itself, the reason we are put on Earth.

In this moment, my father was at peace, the song transporting him to somewhere else, perhaps not even to Jerusalem, but to somewhere higher, to a place where he could be happy. He placed the three *shmura* matzahs at the center of the table. He filled Elijah's cup with wine.

Here, sitting at this table, is the woman who was still legally his wife, as well as his eldest daughter, one of his sons, and three of his grandchildren. Where was he? I thought of the place where my father now lived, the terrible building in North Miami where I'd seen him eight months earlier—alive but eviscerated, suspended between this world and the next. Perhaps it should not have been surprising that my father was drawn to opiates; it was the only way he had left to feel joy.

The Ten Plagues that God inflicted upon the Egyptians came in this order: blood, frogs, lice, wild animals, diseased livestock, boils, hail, locusts, darkness, death of the firstborn. We were no longer living in biblical times, but still, we had our own plagues. The word *Seder* means order. A Seder is meant to give order to suffering, to offer a path toward redemption. But what if there is no redemption? What if the suffering has no end?

I excuse myself from the table and go to the bathroom and lock the door and turn on the faucet. The sound covers the sound of my crying, but only for a short time, because soon my tears become louder than the sound of rushing water. As a teenager, I would give my father pointers after the Seder, suggestions for how to improve the following night. "You should have more participation," I'd tell him. "Ask people questions. People want to know how all this is relevant to their lives." He'd grumble something in his defense and walk away, but the next night he would take my advice.

"How are we each enslaved in our own lives?" he'd ask and give everyone a moment to think.

If you wanted to know how my father was enslaved now, I could tell you that he was enslaved by heroin, by fentanyl, by morphine, by the need to hurt those who cannot fight back, but those were just the presenting facts. The thing that truly enslaved my father was his shame. If he was preying on this girl, it was because he was ashamed. If he was smoking heroin, it was because he was ashamed. If he was alone on Seder night, it was because he was ashamed.

I splash my face with cold water. I let the water run and run and splash my face again.

By the time I return from the bathroom, it is time for "Chad Gadya" ("One Little Goat"). There is no song I love more than this song. It is strange and violent and sad, and even before we start, I know that singing it will make me miss all the things we've lost.

There was one little goat. One very little goat that my father bought for two zuzim. One little goat. One very little goat.

Then came a cat and ate the goat that my father bought for two zuzim. One little goat. One very little goat.

Then came a dog and bit the cat that ate the goat that my father bought for two zuzim.

The song continues in its looping, rhyming logic. A stick comes and beats the dog that bit the cat that ate the goat. Then a fire comes and burns the stick that beat the dog. And on it goes until the Angel of Death comes to kill the slaughterer that killed the ox that drank the water that subdued the fire that burned the stick. It only stops when God arrives to destroy the Angel of Death.

One way to understand the song is that only God has the power to destroy death. God alone has the final word. But here's another way to understand it: This world is populated with predators, that is the nature of things. There is no escape.

15

THE BEGINNING OF COMPASSION

Sara I need help

This message appears on my phone on a Saturday night while I'm watching TV. My husband is out with old friends in from out of town, my son sleeping over at his grandmother's. It is Leah's avatar that appears on my screen, a message from her Facebook account. I think before answering. I wonder if I should answer at all.

Then I write: *What's going on?*

This is Leah's boyfriend
can you send me your number
so we can speak so I can
explain everything to you

It's been months since I've heard from Leah. The last time she messaged me was to say: Fuck ur dad. He ruined everything.

We texted back and forth for days, and I reminded her to stay away from him, to make her safety her top priority.

Before we proceed, it may be worth asking why I was in contact with Leah in the first place. When I called my sister and tried to talk to her about Leah, she would say, "Why are you doing this to yourself? What good will come of this?"

There was pretty much no one who thought it was a good idea. One problem was I was getting more and more depressed. Every time I talked to Leah, I felt worse. A part of me knew that my sister was right—maintaining contact with Leah was not good for me. But another part of me knew she was wrong. If my father was out in the world hurting people, I needed to know about it, I had no choice.

Still, I was tired. I didn't know if I could take in any additional information. I wasn't sure I wanted to know any more than I already knew. I write—

Who is this?? What's happening?

Leah's boyfriend responds that it's too much information to convey over text. He says we need to talk, to have a conversation so he can explain everything. He keeps using that phrase, as though he believes everything can be explained. I hesitate before sending him my number, but I send it anyway. I did not want to look, but I also could not force myself to look away.

On the phone, he tells me Leah is in jail. Also, that she's pregnant. Then he explains everything.

Leah had been arrested for violating her parole, he tells me; the initial charge was shoplifting.

"She wasn't really shoplifting," he tells me. "What happened was she took an iPhone out of someone's cart. She never even left the store!"

According to the boyfriend, Leah's lawyer ("that piece of shit") had dropped her as a client because he wanted her to declare herself mentally unfit to testify, and she'd refused.

"She's not crazy," he says.

"I know that," I say.

"It's all because of what your father did, anyway," he says. "She was never like this before."

The point is, he explains, the hearing is in six weeks. Leah needs a new lawyer, and he wants to know if I can help.

"I've tried," I tell him. "My husband—I've dragged him into this—he's tried too."

I explain everything. How, two years ago, my husband got in touch with a friend of his who is a lawyer in Atlanta, who connected him with a lawyer in Miami who specializes in cases like this one. This lawyer agreed to meet with Leah and review the documents pro bono.

Unfortunately, the lawyer explained, he could not take her on. There was nothing the law could do for her. Leah had signed a release, a release handed to her by the temple's lawyers. A release that offered a cash payout in exchange for her signature. There was no room to maneuver. The agreement was ironclad, the lawyer explained. It waived her rights to ever pursue legal recourse.

"He should be in jail," Leah's boyfriend tells me. "Your father, he should be in jail."

I tell him I agree with him. If I had the power to put my father in jail, I would have done so years ago. So he could never hurt anyone again, not a girl who was his daughter, not a girl who was a congregant. But I don't say that to Leah's boyfriend.

When Leah signed the papers, all parties were absolved. Absolved of accountability, of all further liability. There had never been a criminal case, no official accusations made. I understood that Leah and her boyfriend wanted justice. I wanted justice too. But I did not have the power to dispense it.

"I'm sorry," I tell him. "I wish I could help you, but I don't know how."

"That's okay," he tells me. "At least you tried."

We get off the phone, and I stare at the screen—not the phone screen but the TV screen. I was watching a documentary about a famous musician—a singer, a songwriter, a record-breaking artist. A man so beloved he was nicknamed the Pied Piper. A man whose songs are so uplifting they are sung at graduations and in church. A man who'd been assaulting girls for decades. Some as young as thirteen.

Girl after girl after girl after girl had had her life ruined. The circumstances varied—she'd gone to an audition, a concert, been picked up at her high school—but the results were the same. Who would accuse a good man of such things? A man who'd been singing in the choir since he was a boy, a man who'd given back so much? Only a gold digger. A fame-seeker looking for a payday. A whore.

Yet here they were, on my screen, not one of them, but dozens—girls, now women—showing their faces, saying what happened. The man was not yet in jail; no jury could ever be persuaded. There was always a reasonable doubt, because what reasonable person could believe a man of such talent could be guilty of such things? After every acquittal, he thanked his fans who stood by him with such love, his lawyers, and his friends. Most of all, he thanked God for giving him the strength to get through this.

No mention was ever made of which God the accusers might turn to in their quest for strength, their small scrap of justice. But now, here on my TV screen, was justice of a kind. The kind that comes from telling the truth.

I have just finished putting my son to sleep and am creeping quietly out of his room, when I receive a message on my phone.

> Hi Sara I got out of rehab last week. I did 4 months in jail and 3 months in rehab I was gone for a long time

The message is from Leah. It's been so long since I've heard from her, I didn't know if I'd ever hear from her again.

> Tomorrow god willing I am going to the police station to get the police report to finally show you

> Because I haven't gotten it to you I feel that you think what I said was lies. But as soon as I get it I will show it to you

The police report she is talking about is the same police report she's been talking about since the first time she contacted me, the same police report she's mentioned every time I've spoken with her since, the same police report that describes what happened that night—the first, but not last, time my father assaulted her. For years, she'd been talking about getting a copy, but first she had to go to the police station, first she had to get her head straight.

It had been three years by then, three years I'd been waiting to see the documentation of what my father did. Astonishingly, my father still had his supporters—a coterie of old friends, former congregants, and extended family members—who continued to maintain he was free of any wrongdoing. There was still some piece of me that believed, if we had a piece of paper, some proof that we could point to, somehow that could help, that something could be made right. I never doubted that Leah was telling the truth, but I knew that, without the report, there was no reason anyone else would believe her.

Ten days later, Leah sent me a photograph of the report.

Case Number 2012-51376.

I sit down in the armchair beneath the skylight in the house on the leafy street where my husband and I hope to give our son a happy life. If I look up, I can see the overhanging branches swaying in the white winter sky. As I read, I begin to understand that a police report is just a story, the same as any other story. It's populated by characters, some of whom I recognized, some of whom were new to me.

Take Sergeant P. Wirth #071 and Officer Clair #1010. I'd never heard of them before.

They were the officers who responded to the call, the call from the lobby of my father's apartment building, where a middle-aged woman was screaming that her teenage daughter was upstairs in the rabbi's apartment. The officers rang the doorbell repeatedly, with no answer. But when they knocked on the door, it was opened slightly, with the security chain on the inside of the door in place—and this is where another character enters the story, and that character is my father.

According to the report, my father "appeared to have been drinking and sweating profusely," neither of which were difficult for me to imagine. The report continued:

> As per Sergeant Wirth, he asked the Rabbi if anyone was in his apartment, to which he replied no. When Sergeant Wirth asked the question again, "L" appeared from within the apartment with disheveled clothing and adjusting her bra. "L" also had a strong odor of alcohol about her person. Mr. Sherbill refused to allow any officer to enter his home. All parties were brought to the station for further investigation.

At the station, Leah and my father both gave taped interviews. In her interview, Leah "denied any type of sexual activity with the rabbi and added she is currently menstruating and would not have sex." As for the rabbi—that is, my father—he indicated that the only thing he was guilty of was taking Leah back to his home. He stated they were out talking on his balcony and did not hear the initial knock at the door. He did acknowledge that Leah had been drinking, but refused to discuss how she obtained the drinks or what she drank.

No charges were pressed; no arrest was made. This was the official story, and this was where it ended.

I think of all the times Leah had told me this story—in pieces, in fragments, in broken-off phone calls with months in between. Certain details were the same—that she met with my father to talk, that they went back to his apartment, that it was a warm spring night. But other details were different.

In the story Leah told, it was not alcohol my father gave her, but drugs—though she wasn't sure which ones. In the story Leah told, she passed out, and when she woke up, her dress was hiked up around her hips. In the story Leah told, they weren't just talking on the balcony in the cool evening breeze coming off the ocean. In the story Leah told, my father raped her.

A few minutes later, Leah sends me another text.

Your dad payed them to make this report
The police report is completely altered

I was past trying to guess what my father was or was not capable of. My father was a map whose borders I'd had to draw and redraw so many times that it was impossible to know who or what I was thinking of when I thought of him. The man I'd known— the man I thought was sane enough, discreet enough, to know it is one thing to hurt your own family, something else to hurt strangers—no longer existed.

I thought about the message I'd received from Leah's mother a few months earlier, a text in which she demanded to know why my family had not pressed charges against him years ago, *"knowing that he has been victimizing young women and underage girls??"*

What she didn't understand was that, until three years ago, I had no idea my father had been victimizing young women and underage girls. I always thought the only young woman and underage girl he'd been victimizing was me.

Leah's mother was furious; why shouldn't she be? She is a mother, and it is her right. She wanted a receptacle for her anger. But it could not be me. I didn't blame her for wanting to blame someone, but I could not be that someone.

And, in that moment, I knew that this would be the end of my correspondence with Leah, with her boyfriend, with her mother. They did not owe me any compassion. If I wanted compassion, I was going to have to give it to myself.

I was not the man who did this; I was just his daughter. It was not my obligation to place myself on an altar of suffering to repent for his sins. This was not my fault. None of it was.

When I didn't respond, Leah's mother sent me another text.

Hashem is the lifter of my head!
My family will overcome evil with good.
With God all things are possible—Yeshua the Messiah.

Yeshua, the Hebrew name for Jesus. The term is used exclusively by Messianic Jews, or Jews for Jesus—that is to say, Jews who believe in Christ as their savior. Suddenly I understood. My father's actions had caused Leah's mother to question not just this rabbi or this synagogue, but the nature of God Himself.

I understood her desire to believe in a savior. I also wanted to believe in a savior. I also wanted to believe in a messianic world—a world where kids who seek help from spiritual leaders are not assaulted, a world where religious institutions place the protection of children above all else. But we do not live in that world. If we want a redeemed world, we are going to have to redeem it ourselves.

"I want to write about what happened," I tell Betsy. "Not just to Leah, but to me."

Betsy is my new therapist. She wears high-heeled gladiator sandals and paints her nails fire-engine red. She is probably the most helpful therapist I've ever had.

She nods her head. We have talked about this before.

By then, I'd been writing other people's books for years. Somehow, I had the ability to inhabit another person's voice, to imitate their intonation, to give structure to their story. I just couldn't do it for myself. It was still there languishing—the book I'd been trying to write for years.

Recently, a neurologist contacted me to help him write a book about how he cured himself from a brain tumor. It was a good story, and I needed the work. But every time I thought about doing it, my head felt heavy, and I started to cry. I couldn't write someone else's story again. I was tired of being a ghost. I wanted to be a person.

"I'm afraid I can't do it," I say to Betsy. "I feel like if I haven't been able to do it yet, what makes me think I'm going to be able to do it now?"

"Because it's time," she says. "Because you feel it's time."

16

THE UNBINDING OF ISAAC

IT IS MY MOTHER'S BOYFRIEND who drives us to the courthouse that Friday morning. The three of us in the car, me in the back seat looking out the window, them holding hands in the front. It is still early, and outside the sky is white and foggy.

The courthouse is built in the Greek-revival style, with a colonnade of columns flanking a cobblestone courtyard. I am wearing a white, high-necked blouse tucked into a knife-pleated skirt and high-heeled boots, a pale gray trench coat cinched tightly at the waist, my last defense against whatever may be coming.

My mother's lawyer is waiting for us outside the courtroom. She's promised me the judge's questions will be simple ones. My mother is not asking for anything, neither money nor property, since there are no assets left to divide. As for the children, we are grown and self-sufficient, scattered across the globe. We do not need to prove abuse or addiction or physical danger or mental cruelty. The only thing we need to prove is that my parents have been living apart for more than twelve months. After all this time, that is all we had to prove.

I don't want to be my mother's witness. I am old now and tired of being told my parents' problems are my own. I've moved halfway across the world and back again, moved so many times, trying to get away from this. What my mother doesn't understand is that this is not the first time she is asking me to be a witness. I've already been a witness for so long.

When we enter the courtroom, my mother and I take our seats at the table next to her lawyer, and her boyfriend, Jim, takes a seat in the wooden pews behind us. I've never been inside a secular courtroom before, and it takes a minute to understand what it reminds me of. With its pews and protocols, its hushed fealty to tradition, the courtroom is like a sanctuary, I realize. A place where people come to pray, where they wait for God to determine their fate.

"All rise," the bailiff says, and the judge enters the courtroom in a flowing robe like an ancient high priest. The stenographer takes her place next to the witness stand, ready to record every word that is uttered. Word for word, as it is said, as it is written.

"Good morning, Your Honor," says my mother's lawyer. "Basically, we're here today for in-re divorce. Mr. Sherbill has been in default and has not replied to anything. He has been served every step of the way."

I think of all the things that would enrage my father about the proceedings here today—the fact that my mother has the temerity to divorce him in the first place; that I am there to support her; that she has a boyfriend, and he is here too—the thing that would bother him most is the fact that the lawyer has referred to him as Mr. rather than Rabbi, that she is stealing from him the honor he is due.

"All right," the judge says. "Swear witnesses."

The plaintiff—that is, my mother—is called for examination by counsel.

"You were married to Daniel Sherbill on January 27, 1973, in Chicago, Illinois?"

"Yes."

"You and Daniel were both over eighteen years of age?"

"Yes."

"There were five children born of your marriage, and they are all now emancipated?"

"Yes."

I think about the five children born of this marriage, all now emancipated. My sister, Rachel, who lives with her sixteen-year-old daughter in Tel Aviv; my brother Joseph, who is now divorced and has recently returned from Canada; my brother Ephraim, the only one who stayed in Chicago; the baby, Noam, who has completed nine months of rehab in Southern California, where he is now building a new life from scratch.

The last time we'd all been together was one year earlier, in the fall of 2018, at my mother's seventieth birthday party, held at my home. Everyone—Rachel with her daughter, Joseph, Ephraim with his wife and twins, Noam with his guitar—had flown in from their respective corners of the earth.

My sister's daughter, Eliza, was almost a woman. Unlike me or my sister, she'd inherited my mother's gift of singing. At the end of the night—after I'd strung up lights between two posts in the backyard and put candles in the lanterns, after we'd eaten angel-hair pasta and strawberries with cream under the stars—we went back inside, where Noam and Eliza set up two chairs at the front of the room, while the rest of us gathered on the floor to listen. Noam played guitar, and Eliza sang. I knew this was coming because I'd heard them practicing all afternoon, but I did not expect it to sound like this, like they'd been singing together all their lives, like they'd written every word.

The lawyer asks my mother a few more questions. She wants to confirm she's been a resident of Virginia for at least six months, that the last time she and my father lived together as husband and wife was in Florida, in 2012.

The next witness is called; the next witness is me. But first I have to raise my hand and swear to tell the truth, the whole truth, so help me God.

"Do you know the parties in this divorce action?" the lawyer asks.

"I do."

"How do you know them?"

"They are my parents," I say.

She has more questions.

"Since the date of the separation, to the best of your knowledge and information, have your mom and dad lived separate and apart continuously without cohabitation or interruption?"

"Yes."

"And, to the best of your knowledge and information, your mom formed the intent that the separation would be permanent?"

"Yes."

"And that intention has continued through to the present?"

"Yes."

"In your opinion is there any hope or probability of reconciliation?"

"Absolutely not."

And that is when the judge says: "The divorce is granted."

All my life, my father had threatened that he would never give my mother a divorce according to Jewish law, which, as a man, is his right. But this was not a court of Jewish law; this was the circuit court for the city of Alexandria in the Commonwealth of Virginia. And in order to get a divorce, all my mother had to do was ask.

I lean over to hug my mother, and I can see that she is stunned, too stunned to hug back. There was a time when this would have hurt me or made me angry, the old familiar pattern. But this time, when I look at her, I do not see my mother. I only see a person.

I am forty-three years old the day my parents' divorce is granted. I am no longer a child, so it shouldn't matter, but it does. My whole life, it seemed like nothing could ever change, but now I see that if you keep on living, God rewards you. And if some things can change, maybe everything can change.

In the spring, my brother Noam comes to visit. This time, he does not come alone. He comes with his girlfriend, January, who is four months pregnant, her belly a tiny melon beneath her green floral-print dress. That was the thing about Noam—even in his darkest moments, he'd always talked about wanting to be a father.

When Noam first met January, he was still staying at the sober-living facility where he worked as a manager. It fell to him to drug-test the residents who were there by court order. He had told me some stories. Like the one about the guy who paid good money for bags of clean urine, which he duct-taped to his body and skillfully punctured when he was asked for a sample. Noam was the baby of our family, but it often seemed he knew more about the world than any of us.

When Noam and his girlfriend sit down on my couch, there is no time to waste, so I get down to it.

"What drew you to Noam?" I ask January, and she answers right away.

"His responsiveness," she says. "From the first time he messaged me, he was always right there."

"Plus," she says, smiling at him, "he's a Sagittarius. That's my fire sign."

I don't have to ask what drew Noam to January because it's obvious. She is beautiful, and she is a grown-up with an apartment and a job in marketing who also reads tarot cards and believes that, as human beings, we can tap into the movement of the planets to better understand our life's purpose. Recently, Noam has moved out of the sober-living facility and into January's light-filled apartment not far from the beach. Noam has told me their favorite thing was to go to the farmers market on Sundays to buy fruit and fresh-squeezed juice.

Soon after Noam completed treatment, a friend of his asked if he wanted to go with him to a soundbath. A sound practitioner was playing quartz singing bowls while people lay on the floor, some on mats, some covered in blankets, their eyes closed, letting the sound wash over them. The sound of the crystals and the gong created a warm bath of sound that felt like a cocoon. Noam said it was the most relaxed he had ever felt in his life. A sense of calm had come over him. For the first time, he said, he could feel his body at peace.

After the class, Noam approached the man and asked to apprentice with him. Soon, Noam began working with the man, who promised to teach him all he knew. Noam explained to me how the singing bowls are all tuned to an ancient frequency that can alter our bodies on a cellular level. Before industrialization, all instruments were tuned to this frequency.

"Music has become entertainment," Noam told me. "But its original purpose was to heal."

I understand this is my brother's ancient calling. Sound as ceremony. Sound as medicine.

When Noam and January's baby is born six months later, they give her a name that means *God is with me*. My brother texts me a picture. She is small and dark-haired and perfect. I take the phone and show the picture to my son.

"Look," I tell him, "you have a new baby cousin."

He examines the picture, but doesn't say anything. Then he looks at me and smiles.

I am giving Jonah a bath, and the water is running. There are no dolphins or dinosaurs in the water anymore. He is six now and no longer wants his baby toys.

Instead, he wants to know about my father. Maybe he overheard me on the phone talking to my sister one day, or maybe he heard me talking to my husband when we thought he wasn't listening.

"Do you have a dad, or you don't have a dad?" he asks.

In case it isn't clear, my father is not dead. He's alive and living in North Miami. The last time my son had asked me about my father, I said the reason we don't see him was because he lives in Florida and Florida is too far away. The first half of the sentence was true, but the other half wasn't. Half the time I'd given my son half-truths, the other half I'd trailed off in ellipses. But something had changed. I'd decided I no longer wanted to ever lie to my son about anything.

"I have a dad," I tell him. "He's alive and lives in Florida."

He is looking up at me from the water, his big eyes open, waiting for more.

"The reason we don't see him," I say, "isn't because it's too far away. It's because he's not a nice person. He's done a lot of mean things."

"To who?" my son asks.

And here I must think carefully. I do not want to scare him, but I do not want to lie. My son is looking at me, waiting for an answer.

"He's done mean things to me," I tell him. "And to my brothers and to my sister—and to Ama."

At the mention of his grandmother, my son's eyes widen.

"He has good qualities too," I tell him. "No one is all bad. But I don't believe in having a relationship with someone who is mean to you and to the people that you love."

"Yeah," my son says.

This makes sense to him.

I think about the last time I'd heard from my father, when he sent me an email for my birthday. The note read: *Happy Birthday! Many happy returns.* Signed: *Your father who loves you.* The suggested auto replies included *You're so sweet* and *Thank you!* But I did not reply. It wasn't that I hated my father. I didn't hate him at all. But there was no way I would ever speak to him again, no chance I would let him into my life in even the tiniest of ways. There was too much darkness inside him. I could think about the darkness, I could write about the darkness. But I did not want to touch it, not even from far away.

Every night before bed, I read to my son. Recently we've started reading a book of children's Bible stories. So far, we've covered Adam and Eve, Noah and the Ark, Jonah—my son's namesake—and the whale. Tonight, we are reading the story of the binding of Isaac. Some people call it the sacrifice of Isaac, but that had always bothered me, like they were trying to pretend that Isaac was the one being called upon to make a sacrifice, rather than admitting the sacrifice was him.

I read the words to my son, words that are so foreign to him and so familiar to me.

Some time later God tested Abraham. He said to him,
"Abraham!"
"Here I am," he replied.
Then God said, "Take your son, your only son, whom you love—
Isaac—and go to the region of Moriah. Sacrifice him there as a
burnt offering on a mountain I will show you."

There was a time when I knew these words by heart because I recited them every day as part of the morning prayers. There was a time when I knew these words like the back of my hand, like the back of my mind, where this sliver of knowledge had lodged itself: the knowledge that a child could be sacrificed at any time without warning. That a child could be sacrificed in the name of God, and no one would bat an eye.

My son is confused by the story.

"What's the sacrifice?" he asks me.

"Isaac is the sacrifice," I say.

And his eyes get wider than I've ever seen them.

"No," he says.

He starts to shake his head.

"No," he says again. "This is taking it too far."

I listen to his words, speechless.

"He took it too far," my son says. "He took it too far."

"Who took it too far?" I ask.

And my son says, "God."

It was one thing to say I wanted to write a book. It was another thing to do it. I had come to understand that if I wanted to become the kind of person who could record everything I know, everything I think about, and everything that happens to me without the task eclipsing me, I would need to become a different kind of person.

I would need to learn how to pray again.

I couldn't go back to the old prayers. I would need to learn new ones. I would need new rituals to replace the old.

And so I began by waking up every morning and going for a walk.

After I pack my son's lunch and send him off to school, I lace up my shoes and go into the woods behind our house. In the woods, there's a small footpath that leads to a bigger footpath that goes on for miles. There's a creek nearby, and in the summer, you can hear the water rushing over the rocks.

One morning when I was walking and the sun was hitting through the leaves and the sky was clear and open, I realized something. I was a child who deserved to be protected. I did not deserve to be bound and sacrificed. None of us did.

Before I was my father's child, I was a child of God—a light bigger than my father, bigger than any religion or self-appointed gatekeeper could ever be. Like every soul who enters this world, I was born from the Ein Sof, a power so big we can barely find words to describe it.

Now that I am no longer a child, I have learned some things about God.

*God is not the voice inside your head that tells you you
are bad.*

*God does not care about the length of your hem or the length
of your sleeve.*

God is bigger than that.

God is the voice you can call upon from across a deep chasm.

*God is the thing you draw on when you have nothing left to
draw on. God is the force that tells you you will be okay.*

*God is the power above you, around you, inside you. Wherever
you feel God, that is where God is.*

After my walk, I sit down to write. Every day, I sit down to
write. Even when I do not want to. Even when I have nothing to
say. Still I do it—not out of love, but because I am commanded.
What I have finally come to understand about writing is that it's
a lot like prayer. You may not feel God's presence every time you
pray, but if you keep doing it, you will feel it sometimes.

In the fall, the weather changes. On Friday afternoons, the dark
descends earlier than in the summer, but not as early as when it's
winter. On Friday afternoons, I prepare for the Sabbath. We do
not observe all the laws, nor do we say all the prayers. We do not
go to synagogue, nor do we recite the Grace After Meals. But still,
I prepare for the Sabbath.

I sweep all the floors and make the beds and dust all the book-
shelves. I make chicken and potatoes and soup and set the table
with the dishes we got for our wedding. Maybe my husband buys
me flowers, or maybe he forgets, and I buy them myself and arrange
them in a jar. I place a goblet for the wine on the table and a cutting

board and knife for the bread, because we will bless these things. Because it is the Sabbath and because it is holy.

When it is almost dark, I place the candles in their silver candlesticks, the ones that once belonged to my mother's mother before she died and left my mother alone, and light them with a match. I move my hands from the candles to my eyes in three flowing motions. I place my hands tightly over my eyes and say the prayer silently, almost in my head. Then I say my own prayer, my lips moving, but with no sound coming out.

I kiss my husband, then my son. Then the three of us hug all together.

We bless the wine and the bread. We say the prayers that mark the Sabbath as a remembrance of Creation. We place our hands on our son's head and pray that God will watch over him.

I look at my son's face. My love for my son could fill an ocean, a continent, a book. It could topple a mountain or save a person from a burning building.

"These are rituals," I say to my son. "Do you know what a ritual is?"

He thinks for a moment.

"A ritual is a prayer in visual form," he says.

"That's exactly right," I say.

He is a child, so he understands.

17

APOCRYPHA

WHEN MY FATHER DIED, I did not go to the funeral. Instead, I sat at home and watched through the computer screen as his body was lowered into the ground.

Maybe you could hear my howls as the plain pine coffin was placed into the earth. Maybe you could hear my screams when I realized I would never see my father again.

I did not attend my father's funeral. Neither did my sister or my brother Joseph. But my two youngest brothers were there. Ephraim flew in from Chicago, Noam from LA, to stand at their father's gravesite, shielded by the mangrove trees and weeping willows in the Florida sun.

Because of the pandemic, or perhaps for other reasons, the mourners were sparse. Just my father's remaining relatives and a scattering of former congregants who had since retired to the Sunshine State.

My brothers delivered the eulogies.

Noam talked about how much my father loved music. How he and my father could sit for hours and talk about Neil Young. How music was something they had always shared. He talked about how my father loved to make fruit plates, peeling and slicing mangos and melons and citrus fruits for his children and arranging them on a plate, one of the main ways he showed us his love.

When it was Ephraim's turn, he read from the Book of Ben Sira:

My child, let your tears fall for the dead,
  and as one in great pain begin the lament.
Lay out the body according to custom,
  and do not neglect the burial.
Let your weeping be bitter and your wailing fervent;
  make your mourning worthy of the departed,
for one day or two, to avoid criticism;
  then be comforted for your grief.
For grief may result in death,
  and a sorrowful heart saps one's strength.
. . . .
When the dead are at rest, let their remembrance rest, too,
  and be comforted for them when their spirits have departed.

The Book of Ben Sira is part of the Apocrypha, the body of writings excluded from the Bible. The Apocrypha includes but is not limited to the First Book of Esdras, the Second Book of Esdras, the First Book of the Maccabees, the Second Book of the Maccabees, the chapters from the Book of Esther that were excised from the final text.

You could say that the Apocrypha is comprised of the stories nobody wants to keep but nobody can discard. The stories that somebody, somewhere thought should still be preserved so they could be told.

What about my father's story?

He brought hundreds if not thousands of Jews back to Judaism. He taught them about God and about prayer.

He officiated at weddings and bar mitzvahs and baby namings, blessing every person he encountered.

He gave comfort to mourners. He sat with them and talked with them, and his words gave them solace.

This is the canon of accepted stories, but then there are the other stories. The stories no one wants to tell.

What did my father die of?

By the end, he was suffering from multiple maladies. An advanced form of cancer, a perforated tumor, a Covid diagnosis. His final days were spent in the ICU, isolated from all human contact by layers of plexiglass.

That would have been enough.

But he had also been ingesting opioids for many years, consuming regular and, on some occasions, near-fatal doses of heroin, fentanyl, morphine, oxycodone, whatever was on hand. By the time of his death, he had also been abusing girls for an indeterminate amount of time, at least one whom I knew personally.

Could that be considered a cause of death? The death of the spirit that precedes the death of the body.

Nobody mentioned any of that at my father's funeral, of course. If you want to know those stories, you will need to look elsewhere.

My siblings and I sat shiva on opposite ends of the earth. Rachel and Joseph at Rachel's apartment in Tel Aviv. Ephraim and I at my house in Maryland. Noam with his girlfriend in LA. My mother did not need to sit shiva for my father since she was no longer his wife; she now lived with her boyfriend in the low desert at the foot of the Santa Rosa Mountains.

In the days following my father's death, my sister and brothers and I communicate through a portal that eliminates the space and time between us. In this liminal space, the stories emerge.

Noam tells us about the time he accompanied our father to visit a Holocaust survivor, an old man who lived alone in a tiny apartment on the west side of the city. The man was in a walker and had already lost so much. He kept saying how he wanted to be with his family in the next world, not in this world anymore. He told our father all he wanted was to die.

Noam told us that our father stayed with this man for hours. He spoke to him and listened to him. He held his hand. Maybe that's why our father was drawn to God. Because he knew how painful life on earth was.

But other stories emerge too. Like when a former congregant named Sheldon Winestock showed up at the funeral, and my mother says how strange it is, that he, of all people, would turn up after all these years, since he had called my mother on the phone thirty-five years ago to tell her he had seen the rabbi late one night in a car in the synagogue parking lot with a young woman, a former student, and he thought my mother should know.

It's my mother who tells my sister this story and my sister who tells me.

"What the fuck?" I say to my sister. "I never heard that before."

"What a piece of shit he is," my sister says. "Whatever fruit plate or song he was good for pales in comparison to the girls he assaulted and the family he abused."

These are the stories that emerge only after the dead are buried.

In the days following my father's death, I look him up on the Internet and find his obituary, the accepted story of his life.

Beloved father, brother, friend, and rabbi. Known for his deep knowledge of Judaism, compassion for his congregants and others, and his leadership in interfaith work. He is survived by his five children.

The obituary went on to list our names. There was nothing I could say to argue with that. Even after everything, we were still his children.

Underneath the obituary was a section called "Memories & Condolences." The first entry, written in all caps, described my father as "the kindest of all men."

WHEN MY FATHER WAS DYING 2 YEARS AGO,
IT WAS THE RABBI WHO STAYED ON THE
PHONE WITH ME THROUGH THE END.
HE HAD A HEART AS BIG AS THE SUN.

I did not recognize the name of the person who had penned this message, but I did not doubt its veracity. My entire life people had approached me—in the corridors of the synagogue, over fruit punch and crumbly sprinkle cookies following services—to tell me how much my father had helped them when their loved one passed. Sons, daughters, brothers, sisters, parents who had lost their children. He was there the whole time, holding their hands, talking them through it.

That was my father's gift. He had always been better at death than at life.

When I was young, we marked the borders between sacred and ordinary time. Every Saturday night, once three stars appeared in the night sky, my parents and sister and brothers and I gathered around the havdalah candle. Amid the darkness, save for the glow of the braided candle held aloft in my father's hands, we examined our fingernails against the flame in remembrance of Adam, God's first companion, then said the blessing over the wine, then passed around a small vial filled with cinnamon and cloves that we breathed in to usher in a sweet new week.

My father recites the blessing:

Blessed are You, Lord our God, King of the Universe,
Who separates between the holy and the unholy,
between light and darkness.

Then he spills out the wine and douses the flames. A fiery, crackling sound and a thin plume of smoke rise up as we sing "Shavua Tov," the song that marks the end of sacred time. We hold hands and dance in a circle while we sing. *Elijah the Prophet, Elijah the exalted one.*

I could recite the words of the havdalah ceremony in my sleep, even though I have not recited them in years. It occurs to me that maybe I should say the havdalah blessing now. To mark the time between when my father was alive and the time when he is not. To mark this time in which he's left the earth.

In the weeks following my father's death, my brothers begin attending synagogue again to recite the mourners' kaddish. According to Jewish law, a son is required to recite the kaddish with a quorum every day for the eleven months following a parent's death. For a split second, in the wake of my father's death, I wonder whether I should do the same.

But then I remember that I had already recited kaddish at my father's funeral. Just after his body was lowered into the ground,

I stood alone in front of the computer screen and whispered the prayer for the dead.

I think of how many times I'd heard this prayer, how I could never imagine saying the words myself. According to tradition, it is the recitation of the kaddish that elevates the soul of the deceased, that ensures its passage from this world to the next. I am my father's daughter, and I know this is my job.

But I already said the words once, and I cannot say them again.

Instead, I think about the photograph my mother texted me not long ago. A black-and-white photograph of me and my father taken at the Dead Sea, the lowest place on earth, when I am one year old.

In the picture, my father is wearing a large embroidered skullcap and an untended beard, the markers of a religious man. I think of the person my father was when he first came to Jerusalem, after dropping out of college and drifting around Mexico. It was 1970 or '71, and young people had flooded the city, college students and dropouts and hippies and druggies and former druggies and children of Holocaust survivors, all dreaming of transcendence.

He was young then, looking for credibility and purpose, something commensurate with his intellect, something that would command the respect he was due. If he became a man of God, it would solve several problems at once. Or maybe it was purer than that. Maybe for a time my father believed that, by saving other people, he might save himself.

In the photograph my mother sends me, my eyes peer out from under a white muslin cloth placed over my head to protect me from the sun. In the photograph, my father is holding me, holding me so close he will never let me go.

ACKNOWLEDGMENTS

The fact that this book exists is testament to three extraordinary women: My agent, Jöelle Delbourgo, who instinctively understood what this book could be and through her guidance and expertise helped me to get it there. My editor, Jane Rosenman, who taught me more about how to shape a story than I ever hoped to learn; this book would not exist without her. And my editor at Union Square & Co., Barbara Berger, who resonated with this story immediately and had the courage to champion it; I am thankful my story found its way to her.

Thank you to my mom, who has shown me through her courage and beauty how to change your life—thank you for listening, for supporting this book, and for always being there. To my sister and brothers, my heart and soul—thank you for living this story with me and for supporting my telling it. 1850 Forever.

Thank you to Aliza Hakimian, healer, guide, and forever best friend—you are always with me. Thank you to Jennifer Sitron for so much laughter over so many years. Thank you to Shelley Klein for being my home away from home. Thank you to Bryce Jacobs, my girl in DC. Thank you to longtime friends Dara Grossman, Deena Birnbaum, Michal Skarf, Dalia Nagel, Michael Kaufman, and Rachel Loren. Thank you to Nicole Drexler, my touchstone.

Thank you to the editors who have published my work, especially Jodi Rudoren at the *Forward*; Alana Newhouse at *Tablet*; and Dan Kois at *Slate*, who understood the importance of revisiting Hedda Nussbaum's story and whose exquisite editing helped bring it to life.

Thank you to the late Ashbel Green for hiring me at Knopf, for teaching me how to edit, and for showing me so much kindness. I am grateful to the teachers who have encouraged my writing, especially Mary Gordon, in whose classes the earliest version of this book first took shape. Thank you for teaching me so much about how to read and how to write, and for believing in me as a writer.

Thank you to Ariel Burger, generous reader and true friend. Thank you to Mark Benjamin for his friendship and help. Thank you to Elisabeth Fink Benjamin for her brilliant eye. Thank you to Lisa Forde for the gorgeous cover.

Thank you to Chedva, my light and inspiration—thank you for leading the way for the next generation. Special thanks to Candice Na for her help and guidance, and for believing in this book. Thank you to Dennis Ritchie for his love and support.

Thank you to Rafael, my shining star, who changed everything. Thank you for being who you are and for teaching me so much. My love for you is infinite.

Finally, to Charlie. You believed in this book from the beginning. You never wavered. For this and for so many other gifts you have brought into my life, I am forever grateful.